A STUDY GUIDE TO THE

Facsimiles

OF THE BOOK OF ABRAHAM

A STUDY GUIDE TO THE

Facsimiles

OF THE BOOK OF ABRAHAM

By Allen J. Fletcher

CFI
Springville, Utah

ISBN 13: 978-1-55517-931-2
ISBN 10: 1-55517-931-2
c. 2

Published by CFI, an imprint of Cedar Fort, Inc., 925 N. Main, Springville, UT, 84663
Distributed by Cedar Fort, Inc. www.cedarfort.com

Cover design by Nicole Williams
Cover design © 2006 by Lyle Mortimer
Printed in the United States of America

10   9   8   7   6   5   4   3   2

Printed on acid-free paper

TABLE OF CONTENTS

ACKNOWLEDGMENTS

I give heartfelt thanks to Vernon Jubber for his undying support and assistance in this project. I give special thanks to my father, Nyal A. Fletcher, for his assistance and encouragement over the years. I thank Rick Cartier. I thank my daughter Marina for helping to verify all the references. Finally, I give appreciation and thanks to my wife, Elaine, who has spent many long hours proofreading and checking references, and much time alone while I completed this work. She has given me every possible consideration of time and energy; she is my confidante, sounding board, and dearest friend.

PREFACE

The Facsimiles of the Book of Abraham
A Brief Historical View of the Book of Abraham

Egyptian Papyri Possessed by Joseph Smith

Neither time nor space is available in a small work such as this for a close consideration of the history of the Book of Abraham; however, a brief review of the account is required to appreciate the miracle associated with these profound materials. This background information is intended to establish a suitable climate for discussing the three Abrahamic facsimiles.

From an Egyptian Tomb

With the fall of the great Napoleonic army at Waterloo, many Europeans seeking further adventure made their way to Egypt, intending to steal the nation's ancient treasures for profit. Egypt was technologically backward in the early nineteenth century, and to obtain "industrial assistance, Mehemet Ali [viceroy of Egypt] allowed the European visitors to rob graves and plunder the relics of Egypt's illustrious past." In the early

1820s, a dig in the Necropolis of Thebes resulted in the find of several hundred mummies, eleven of which were extracted by dig supervisor Antonio Lebolo. Through a series of incidents, most of which remain a mystery, the eleven mummies arrived in New York City sometime in early 1833 and came into the possession of a new proprietor, Michael H. Chandler (Peterson, *The Pearl of Great Price*, 38–41).

Chandler Arrives in Kirtland

Michael Chandler took the mummies on tour, charging twenty-five cents admission to view the exhibit. The first showing of record was held in Philadelphia in April 1833. By March 1835, Chandler had sold seven of the eleven mummies to various purchasers, and in July he traveled to Kirtland, Ohio, where the Prophet Joseph Smith was residing. Joseph, upon viewing the papyrus documents, was impressed to purchase them from Chandler, who refused to sell the scrolls without the mummies. Joseph, Simon Andrews, Joseph Coe, and some others obtained the necessary funds and purchased the mummies and papyrus for $2,400. (See Peterson, *The Story of the Book of Abraham*, 6.)

Joseph Smith, in summarizing the miracle of receiving these things, recorded, "Soon after this, . . . with W. W. Phelps and Oliver Cowdery as scribes, I commenced the translation of some of the characters or hieroglyphics, and much to our joy found that one of the rolls contained the writings of Abraham, another the writings of Joseph of Egypt, etc. . . . Truly we can say, the Lord is beginning to reveal the abundance of peace and truth" (Joseph Smith, *History of the Church*, 2:236).

Joseph Smith Publishes the Book of Abraham

Joseph's work on the ancient documents continued over the next seven years and culminated with the serial publishing of the current text of the Book of Abraham in the *Times and Seasons* between March 1, 1842 and May 16, 1842.

In the February 1, 1843, edition of the *Times and Seasons*, John Taylor reported that Joseph Smith had promised "to furnish us with further extracts from the Book of Abraham" (Peterson, *The Story of the Book of Abraham*, 153). Unfortunately, he was never afforded the opportunity to do so prior to his martyrdom in 1844.

After the Martyrdom

Following the martyrdom, the mummies and the papyrus documents were left in the care of Lucy Mack Smith, Joseph's mother, and she for some time displayed the materials as a modest means of income. Shortly after his excommunication in 1845, William Smith, Joseph's brother, retrieved the mummies and papyrus from his mother and used them for a time in a traveling lecture series he organized. Although the details remain obscure, the mummies and papyrus were eventually sold to a Mr. Abel Combs, and subsequently some of the collection was sold to the St. Louis Museum. The mummies were later moved to the Chicago Museum (later called the Wood's Museum), where they were kept until their presumed destruction in the Chicago fire of 1871.

Valuable Discovery of 1967

In 1967 several of the original papyrus manuscripts were discovered by University of Utah professor Dr. Aziz S. Atiya in the Metropolitan Museum of Art in New York City; they were presented to the Church on November 27 that year. Apparently Mr. Combs, who purchased the mummies from members of the Smith family, had retained some of the documents and left them to a servant, a Mrs. Heusser, in his will. She in turn left the documents to her daughter upon her passing. Mrs. Heusser's son-in-law then sold the documents to the museum in 1946. Some speculation exists regarding the survival and existence of other original documents and manuscripts, including the original manuscript of Joseph Smith's translation of the Book of Abraham.

Special Challenge

The study of the Book of Abraham, and especially the facsimiles, has from the beginning been a challenging endeavor. The intent of this work is to examine each facsimile in an attempt to help the reader see things in them that will increase their faith and testimony of Abraham, Joseph Smith, and the Savior.

CHAPTER 1

The Mission of Abraham to Egypt

The Journey Begins

To understand more of the value and significance of the three facsimiles in the Book of Abraham, let us begin by following Abraham on his journey from Ur of the Chaldees down into the land of Egypt.

When his record opens, we find Abraham, in Ur, righteously seeking for the blessings of the priesthood.

> In the land of the Chaldeans, at the residence of my fathers, I, Abraham, saw that it was needful for me to obtain another place of residence;
>
> And, finding there was greater happiness and peace and rest for me, I sought for the blessings of the fathers, and the right whereunto I should be ordained to administer the same; having been myself a follower of righteousness, desiring also to be one who possessed great knowledge, and to be a greater follower of righteousness, and to possess a greater knowledge, and to be a

father of many nations, a prince of peace, and desiring to receive instructions, and to keep the commandments of God, I became a rightful heir, a High Priest, holding the right belonging to the fathers.

It was conferred upon me from the fathers; it came down from the fathers, from the beginning of time, yea, even from the beginning, or before the foundation of the earth, down to the present time, even the right of the firstborn, or the first man, who is Adam, or first father, through the fathers unto me.

I sought for mine appointment unto the Priesthood according to the appointment of God unto the fathers concerning the seed. (Abraham 1:1–4)

When he had obtained the priesthood, Abraham explains that through his preaching, he became a threat to his father and the other wicked priests who were all worshipping idols. He said they "utterly refused to hearken to my voice; for their hearts were set to do evil" (Abraham 1:5–6). He explains that he was taken by these wicked priests and placed upon an altar of death. Next he describes his miraculous delivery from the altar and from the hands of the wicked priests. "And as they lifted up their hands upon me, that they might offer me up and take away my life, behold, I lifted up my voice unto the Lord my God, and the Lord hearkened and heard, and he filled me with the vision of the Almighty, and the angel of his presence stood by me, and immediately unloosed my bands" (Abraham 1:15).

After this terrifying experience, Abraham is commanded to leave his residence at Ur and flee into a land then unknown to him. "Behold, my name is Jehovah, and I have heard thee, and have come down to deliver thee, and to take thee away from thy father's house, and from all thy kinsfolk, into a strange land which thou knowest not of" (Abraham 1:16).

Abraham tells of a great famine that came upon the land and in the midst of that famine, he with his wife and some of his family left his homeland behind. He describes their journeys from place to place until they finally arrived at a mountain east of Bethel, where they pitched their tents and offered sacrifice unto the Lord. The Lord appeared to Abraham during his journeys and made covenants with him and gave to him and his posterity the land of Canaan for an everlasting inheritance. He continues with his narrative. "There was a continuation of a famine in the land; and I, Abraham, concluded to go down into Egypt, to sojourn there, for the famine became very grievous" (Abraham 2:21).

During these travels, a great vision of the Lord opened unto him. He saw many of the creations of God and beheld God's great glory. He was shown the stars and planets and the intelligences that were organized before the world was. He explains that during the course of this vision, the Lord said, "I show these things unto thee before ye go into Egypt, that ye may declare all these words" (Abraham 3:15).

Onward to the Borders of Egypt

Armed with that commandment and with that information, Abraham departed with his family and headed into Egypt. We might wonder what Abraham was thinking as he approached the Egyptian border and how in the world he, a person whom the Egyptians hated and had recently tried to kill, would ever find himself in a position to instruct such people. He must have felt much like Nephi approaching Laban to get the plates of brass: " I was led by the Spirit, not knowing beforehand the things which I should do" (1 Nephi 4:6).

We learn that it was through Sarah that the way was opened for Abraham to teach the pharaoh. Sarah was commanded to tell the pharaoh that she was Abraham's sister, and the pharaoh tried to take her for a wife. When he did so, he was struck down by an angel so that he could not approach her. Sarah finally told him that Abraham was her husband, and when Abraham was summoned, as the story goes, he laid his hands on the head of pharaoh and healed him. Of course, this created quite a stir, and the result was that Abraham was invited to sit on the throne of pharaoh and teach his people (see Abraham 2:22–25; Genesis 12:13–19; *The Book of Jasher*, 38–39; Fitzmyer, *The Genesis Apocryphon*, 53, 55–57, 59).

What of the Facsimiles?

In some way connected with his mission to Egypt, Abraham possessed and preserved three curious Egyptian documents that have found their way into our scriptures. Hugh Nibley said, "The facsimiles were originally intended as visual aids . . . nothing supernatural, inspired, or sacrosanct is claimed for them" (Nibley, "As Things Stand at the Moment," *BYU Studies*, 95). These were not unique to Abraham or even necessarily his original work but were, "thoroughly conventional representations of well-known Egyptian scenes, identical copies of which could be produced in unlimited quantities . . . a series of documents which were common property of a whole nation of people who employed them in every human burial, which they prepared" (Nibley, "A New Look at the Pearl of Great Price," *Improvement Era,* September 1968, 66).

Why would Abraham preserve such documents? What message do they contain that would make them valuable to him? And perhaps more important: who were the Egyptians, and what were they doing that caused them to produce documents that would be of value to Abraham?

An Earnest Imitation

The answers to these questions are found in the nature of Egyptian theology. In order to understand and appreciate that theology, we must return to the account of Abraham.

Of Abraham's calling to the priesthood, the scriptures say:

1. He sought for the blessings of the fathers and the right to be ordained to administer those blessings.
2. That he was a follower of righteousness.
3. That he desired to be "a father" and "a prince of peace."
4. That he became a high priest, holding the right that came down from the fathers, the right of the Firstborn even of Adam, the first father (see Abraham 1:2–4).

Other scriptures expand and clarify this right. Alma says that it came from God and was "after his holy order, which was after the order of his Son," "a holy calling," "the high priesthood of the holy order of God," and that "ordinances were given after this manner, that thereby the people might look forward on the Son of God," and that by this right, "Melchizedek was a king over the land of Salem," and "he was called the prince of peace" (see Alma 13:1–19). The Doctrine and Covenants, speaking of Adam who held this right, says that he was "the father of all, the prince of all, the ancient of days" (D&C 27:11). Speaking of Christ as the author of this right, Isaiah says, "his name shall be called Wonderful, Counsellor, The mighty God, The everlasting Father, The Prince of Peace" (Isaiah 9:6). And finally, the book of Revelation says that those holding this right become "kings and priests unto God" (Revelation 1:6).

From the foregoing we glean the following:

1. The right which Abraham speaks about is the holy order of the Son of God, which was prepared from before the foundation of the world, and was the right of the Firstborn, coming down to others through Adam, the first father or ancient of days.

-4-

2. Those who possess this holy order are high priests, even kings and priests unto God. They are, by inference, associated with temples.
3. This holy order was given in a manner that by it, or through it, the people might look forward to the Atonement of Jesus Christ. And this was because it was given in the beginning before He would come in the flesh to make intercession for all men. This, of course, suggests the idea that the ancient fathers, in their day, participated in ordinances or performances that pointed to the coming of Christ in the future.
4. Those who possess this order, take upon them the name of Christ, which is evidenced by the name which Adam, Abraham, and Melchizedek received, even the title Prince or Prince of Peace, which Isaiah says is the name of Christ (see Isaiah 9:6).

In the light of these things, it is instructive to review the Prophet Joseph's account of introducing, for the first time in this dispensation, the temple endowment in his red-brick store in Nauvoo on May 3, 1842. Joseph says that he spent the day in the upper part of the store, in council with certain brethren, "instructing them in the principles and order of the Priesthood, attending to washings, anointings, endowments and the communication of keys pertaining to the Aaronic Priesthood, and so on to the highest order of the Melchizedek Priesthood setting forth the order pertaining to the Ancient of Days, and all those plans and principles by which anyone is enabled to secure the fulness of those blessings which have been prepared for the Church of the Firstborn, and come up and abide in the presence of the Eloheim in the eternal worlds. In this council was instituted the ancient order of things for the first time in these last days" (Smith, *History of the Church*, 5:1–2).

Here we see exactly what Abraham and the other prophets were referring to when they spoke of the right to hold that holy order of God, which came down from the beginning even through Adam. Accordingly, those who were here first endowed by Joseph were organized into a quorum and were referred to variously as the Holy Order or the Ancient Order (Ehat, *Joseph Smith's Introduction of Temple Ordinances,* 101).

Now we come to the heart of the matter concerning the beliefs of the Egyptians to whom Abraham was sent. Of them he says, "Pharaoh, being a righteous man, established his kingdom and judged his people wisely and justly all his days, seeking earnestly to imitate that order established by the fathers in the first generations, in the days of the first patriarchal reign, even in the reign of Adam, and also of Noah, his father, who blessed him with the blessings of the earth, and with the blessings of wisdom, but cursed him as pertaining to the Priesthood" (Abraham 1:26).

We can scarcely imagine the depth of what Abraham is telling us in this verse. He is saying, in effect, that the pharaohs in their theology were practicing the principles of the true and ancient order that were established in the beginning with Adam and Noah. He was even kind enough to tell us how they got that theology—it was, he says, from the first pharaoh through his mother (Egyptus), who was the daughter of Ham (see Abraham 1:25), the son of Noah. This lineage was not the patriarchal line through which priesthood was authorized (see Abraham 1:26–27); therefore rather than possessing its blessings, they earnestly imitated its performances. The word imitate is not a negative here. Rather, it represents an affection and longing for, and an attention to detail, hoping that if enough energy and devotion were spent, it might work, after all.

So where would we turn in Egyptian theology to see this imitation? Remember it would involve the idea of the following things:

1. The holy order of the Son of God, and an idea of Adam, the first father or ancient of days, and the right of the Firstborn.
2. High priests, even kings and priests, associated with temples.
3. Ordinances or performances that point to Christ.
4. The principle of individuals taking upon themselves the name of Christ.

If I might be so bold as to say, that is Egyptian theology! They had their own names for it's elements, and their own ways of presenting it, but a little examination soon shows up the imitation.

A Brief Look at Egyptian Theology

With the conquest of Egypt by the early kings of the First Dynasty, new views as to the future life appear to have entered the country, and resulted in the belief that a certain man who had lived and died upon earth had, by some means, raised himself up to life again and succeeded in making himself the god of the dead. The inscriptions of the first three dynasties tell us nothing about his being, and though certain incidents in his life are referred to by the writers of the texts of the IVth dynasty, it is not until we come to the connected religious compositions of the Vth and VIth dynasties that we obtain any definite statements about him. The details of the history of the remarkable being who had risen from the dead were assumed by the scribes to be so well-known that they are not described in the great religious compositions that have come down to us.

Only by piecing together the information given here and there can we arrive at any connected views of what happened to him, and to this day, in spite of the mass of religious and magical literature available, we are wholly ignorant of the origin and general history of the first human being in Egypt who rose from the dead, and who was known for thousands of years as Khenti-Amenti, or Chief of those who are in the Other World.

Of the home of this being who rose from the dead, and of the position which he occupied in this world, nothing can be learned from the texts. However, late Greek writers assert that he was a king. The exact region in Egypt where his kingdom was situated is unknown. And the name of this man was Osiris, in Egyptian *Asar* (Budge, *Osiris and the Egyptian Resurrection,* 1:66).

Asar, Osiris

Of Osiris, Bonwick says, "His birth, death, burial, resurrection and ascension embraced the leading points of Egyptian theology" (Bonwick, *Egyptian Belief and Modern Thought,* 150). Let's compare some of that theology to the points we outlined above.

1. The right that Abraham speaks about is the holy order of the Son of God, which was prepared from before the foundation of the world and was the right of the Firstborn, coming down to others through Adam, the first father or ancient of days.

Osiris was thought to have had an existence before his physical birth and in that realm attained a state of godhood: "Whilst thou wert in the womb and hadst not as yet come forth therefrom upon the earth, thou wert crowned Lord of the two lands, and the Atef crown of Ra was upon thy brow. The gods come unto thee bowing low to the ground, and they hold thee in fear; they retreat and depart when they see thee possessing the terror or Ra, and the victory of thy Majesty is in their hearts" (Budge, *The Gods of the Egyptians*, 2:159).

He was called the Firstborn of God. His father was Ra, the god of heaven. "I am the firstborn of the primeval god, and my soul is the Souls of the Eternal Gods, and my body is Everlastingness. My created form is [that of] the god Eternity, the Lord of Years, and the Prince of Everlastingness. I am the Creator of the Darkness, who maketh his seat in the uttermost limits of the heavens, [which] I love" (Budge, *The Book of the Dead*, 550).

"Osiris sits on the Great Throne by the side of the Great God. He is God, the firstborn of the firstborn" (Budge, *Osiris and the Egyptian Resurrection*, 1:119, 121).

"Ra was held to be the father of Osiris" (Budge, *The Gods of the Egyptians*, 2:141).

It was claimed that Osiris' "kingly" descent was from the first man of the race—the Ancient One, or Ancient of Days, the first king.

"Osiris is called the son of Atum" (Griffiths, *The Origins of Osiris and His Cult,* 15). The royal line begins with "Atum, the very Old One [Adam the Ancient of Days] . . . assimilated to Hr [Horus] as the ruler of Egypt and the heavenly god" (Nibley, *Abraham in Egypt*, 215). The name Atum signified both the Creator and "the collective sum of all future beings," "the Ancient One" par excellence, the Ancient One with whom the genealogy of the race begins (Nibley, *The Message of the Joseph Smith Papyri*, 133, 241–42).

The king wears the "patriarchal Crown of the Father of the gods" (Nibley, *Abraham in Egypt*, 179). "As Prince of gods and men thou hast received the crook, and the whip, and the dignity of his divine fathers" (Budge, *The Gods of the Egyptians*, 2:153).

Osiris claimed the priesthood, and the kings who worshipped him held his priesthood also. It was a priesthood that had come down from Atum, the first man.

The crown of Osiris represented the priesthood (see Facsimile 3: Figure 1). The king was a high priest (Griffiths, *The Origins of Osiris and His Cult*, 4). The pharaoh was also a king and a priest. He was the official high priest of Heliopolis and every other temple in Egypt. His crown is the two-plumed *atef,* a symbol of power, priesthood, light, and holiness (Harris, "The Book of Abraham Facsimilies," 2:245). In Egypt, "it is not possible for a king to rule without the priesthood."

The king officiated at Heliopolis in the capacity of a priest "That the King should be a High Priest seems almost incomprehensible to us . . . but it was the combining of these (royal and priestly) powers that was the Key" to everything. "I give to thee the throne of Geb (the primal earth-father), and the office of Atum (Adam)." "I (Amon the father of the gods) give to thee my seat of inheritance under me. . . . I am thy beloved father who establishes thy authority (sah) . . . who confirms thy titles." In the Pyramid Texts the right to rule is established by formal demonstration of patriarchal descent from Geb. The Egyptians always trace their royal authority to the pawt, "primaeval time, the beginning of time"; for them, "a man of ancient family" is a pawty. The king is "foreordained (sr) to the throne of Geb (the primal ances-tor, the principle of patriarchal succession), and the office of Khpri (the principle of ongoing creation), at the side of my Father (Amon)" (Nibley, *Abraham in Egypt,* 83–86).

2. Those who possess this holy order are high priests, even kings and priests unto God. They are, by inference, associated with temples.

The priesthood of the Egyptians was organized for temple worship.

"To be sure one of the fundamental duties of the Egyptian king was the building of temples and offering of sacrifices. . . . He performs this function as son of the gods, who in a very special way have granted him life" (Keel, *The Symbolism of the Biblical World,* 269).

"As builder of the temple the king is responsible for its maintenance and for the cultus which is carried on in it. The concentration of the kingly and priestly offices in a single person [links to] the prototype, Melchizedek, who was simultaneously king and priest of the highest god" (Genesis 14:18—the 'most high God')" (Keel, *The Symbolism of the Bibli-cal World,* 277).

"According to the relief cycles, it is the Pharaoh who daily opens the holy of holies and venerates the god, his father. . . .

"Obviously, it was necessary for the king to delegate his priestly func-tions, except on special occasions. Still, the priests served under his com-mission" (Keel, *The Symbolism of the Biblical World,* 279).

The daily rites performed in all Egyptian temples, in the king's name and at his expense, were conducted in the innermost shrine and in secret (Montet, *Everyday Life in Egypt,* 280).

3. This holy order was given in a manner that by it, or through it, the

people might look forward to the Atonement of Jesus Christ. And this was because it was given in the beginning before He would come in the flesh to make intercession for all men. This, of course, suggests the idea that they, the ancient fathers, in their day, participated in ordinances or performances that pointed to the coming of Christ in the future.

- "The baptism of Egypt is known by the hieroglyphic term of 'waters of purification.' In Egypt, the water so used in immersion absolutely cleansed the soul, and the person was said to be regenerated" (Bonwick, *Egyptian Belief and Modern Thought*, 416)
- "The Eucharist (sacrament) was known in Egypt. As it is recognized that the bread after sacerdotal rites becomes mystically the body of Osiris; in such manner, they ate their god. Doubtless the better informed held that the elements by prayer were so powerfully endowed with supernatural grace as to affect the soul's growth into the very nature of the gods. The cakes of Osiris were round, and they were placed upon the altar. 'The Egyptians marked this holy bread with St. Andrew's cross.' The Presence bread was broken before being distributed by the priests to the people and was supposed to become the flesh and blood of the Deity. The miracle was wrought by the hand of the officiating priest, who blessed the food. Another interesting parallel may be mentioned here: 'The cakes . . . were not only eaten from the hand of the priest, but were taken to persons unable to be present'" (ibid., 416–18).
- "'When one is baptized one becomes a Christian,' writes Cyril, 'exactly as in Egypt by the same rite one becomes an Osiris.' Not only does Cyril recognize the undeniable resemblance between the Christian and non-Christian rites, but he also notes that they have the identical significance that is initiation into immortality. Temple worship: Cyril speaks of another baptism, which is rather a washing than a baptism, since it is not by immersion. It is followed by an anointing, which our guide calls 'the antitype of the anointing of Christ himself,' making every candidate as it were a Messiah. Elsewhere, he describes this rite specifically as the anointing of the brow, face, ears, nose, breast, and so forth, 'which represents,' he says,

'the clothing of the candidate in the protective panoply of the Holy Spirit' but does not hinder the initiate from receiving a real garment on the occasion. Furthermore, the candidate was reminded that the whole ordinance 'is an imitation of the sufferings of Christ,' in which 'we suffer without pain by mere imitation his receiving of the nails in his hands and feet: the antitype of Christ's sufferings'" (Madsen, *The Temple in Antiquity*, 27).

4. Those who possess this order, take upon them the name of Christ, which is evidenced by the name Adam, Abraham, and Melchizedek received, even the title Prince or Prince of Peace, which Isaiah says is the name of Christ.

- "How great art thou, O King. . . . Thy name is raised to that of Osiris" (Griffiths, *The Origins of Osiris and His Cult*, 229).
- "Thou art a king, because thou art not to be distinguished from Osiris" (Nibley, *The Message of the Joseph Smith Papyri*, 150).
- "I am the firstborn of the primeval god, and my soul is the Souls of the Eternal Gods, and my body is Everlastingness. My created form is [that of] the god Eternity, the Lord of Years, and the Prince of Everlastingness" (Budge, *The Book of the Dead*, 550).
- "As Prince of gods and men thou hast received the crook, and the whip, and the dignity of his divine fathers" (Budge, *The Gods of the Egyptians*, 2:153).
- "Osiris . . . was the Divine healer and the Good Physician, the Prince of Peace and goodwill, the Manifestor of the Ever Hidden Father, and Builder of the Temple of Peace" (Baily, *The Lost Language of Symbolism*, 1:160).
- The aim of every good man was to become an Osiris, and even in the Pyramid Texts, we find it tacitly assumed that the kings for whom they were written had each become an Osiris; in fact, the name of Osiris is actually prefixed to some of their names (Budge, *Osiris and the Egyptian Resurrection*, 2:2–3).

Although the doctrine of Osiris and his life and mission were celebrated from the beginning of Egyptian history, no one could say exactly when or where he was born or where he lived. They knew of his life and death and the fact that "at the end of three days . . . he rose again, and ascended to heaven" (Bonwick, *Egyptian Belief and Modern Thought,* 155), but they could not find in him a historical figure. This point is expressed by Bonwick, who observed that the life and mission of Christ and Osiris were so parallel that "some may be disposed to think that the Egyptians being aware of the promises of the real Savior, had anticipated that event, regarding it as though it had already happened, and introduced that mystery into their religion" (*Egyptian Belief and Modern Thought,* 183).

How the Egyptians could have known of the "promises of the real Savior," he does not say, but all this surely points to what Abraham calls an "earnest imitation" by the pharaohs.

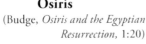

Osiris
(Budge, *Osiris and the Egyptian Resurrection,* 1:20)

Christ

The question we now address is what all this has to do with Abraham possessing and preserving the facsimiles. Let's look at each of the three documents to determine what is going on in them. What are their messages? What are they about? The more we study them, the more we discover that they share one Egyptian theological theme: Osiris.

A Facsimile from the Book of Abraham, No. 1

If viewed strictly as an Egyptian document, Facsimile 1 is a fairly typical scene depicting the death and resurrection of the god Osiris. Other scenes much like this depict the same basic theme.

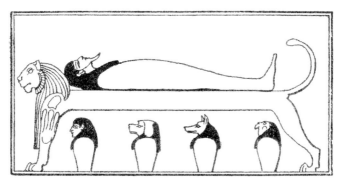

Osiris on his bier under which are the vases containing his intestines.
Mariette, *Dendérah*, IV, 70.

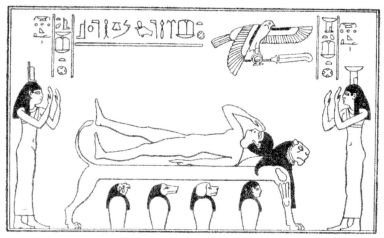

Osiris, Isis, and Nephthys of the town of Hebit (Behbît).   Above is a hawk
bringing air.

Mariette, *Dendérah*, IV, 72.

(Budge, *Osiris and the Egyptian Resurrection,* 2:39)

"[These] pictures are telling us more than just what happened at one moment. [Each] picture recounts a whole series of events. The man on the couch is in great distress, he has been beaten by his enemy, he is on the point of death; he cries out to his father . . . to come to his aid, and sure enough, there is . . . the bird flying above him. The hawk Horus has come to rescue (him) from death" (Nibley, "A New Look at the Pearl of Great Price," *Improvement Era,* May 1969, 90). In another scene, "He is just about to get up and dress, in fact, look how 'below the bed there are spread out the royal regalia . . . of which (he) would presently take possession after his rebirth'" (ibid., 91).

This is the atef crown Osiris will assume as he takes his place as 'Khnum' in the center of the Universe (Figure 1 in Facsimile No. 2)

(Budge, *Osiris and the Egyptian Resurrection,* 2:43)

The resurrection of Osiris Khenti-Àmenti.
Mariette, *Dendérah*, IV, 90.

14

Facsimile No. 2

As Osiris arises from the dead, he takes his place at the center of the universe, as represented by Figure 1 in our Facsimile No. 2. That center is represented by showing Osiris between two goddesses, Isis and Nephthys (shown as apes of the dawn in our Figure 1)—the two eternities (Nibley, *The Message of the Joseph Smith Papyri,* 116). Osiris can be shown with one, two, or four ram heads. In the Hypocephali, he is most often shown with four, associated with the four canopic gods and representing the four elements or the four directions (Nibley, "A New Look at the Pearl of Great Price," *Improvement Era,* August 1969, 82).

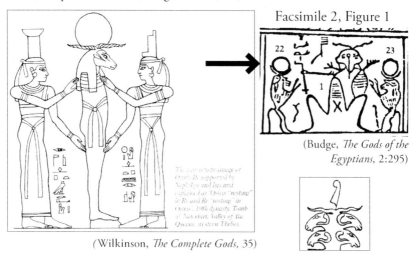

Facsimile 2, Figure 1

(Budge, *The Gods of the Egyptians,* 2:295)

(Wilkinson, *The Complete Gods,* 35)

The ram appears in the center of nearly every Hypocephalus.

(Birch, *Proceedings,* 6:106)

Having identified Facsimile No. 2 with Osiris, let us examine how thoroughly it is a document about him. How many places in Facsimile No. 2 do we find references to Osiris?

1. Khnum (a form of Osiris) (Rhodes, *The Joseph Smith Hypocephalus*, 7).
2. The name of the dead as an initiate, having taken upon himself the name Osiris (ibid., 5).
3. A prayer to Osiris, the Mighty God, "Lord of heaven, earth, netherworld, the great waters" (Rhodes, *The Joseph Smith Hypocephalus*, 5). These, in principle, relate to the four heads of Osiris as earth, fire, water, and air.
4. Osiris as Seker a manifestation of death and resurrection (Budge, *The Gods of the Egyptians*, 1:507).
5. A promise given that the initiate will become as Osiris (Rhodes, *The Joseph Smith Hypocephalus*, 5).
6. Djabty, the mighty god, Osiris (ibid., 4).
7. The Name of the mighty god, which is Osiris (Rhodes, *The Joseph Smith Hypocephalus*, 5).
8. Amun-Ra, a composite god who identifies with Osiris (Nibley,

The Message of the Joseph Smith Papyri, 249, 134).

9. The mighty god in Heliopolis, who is Osiris (Rhodes, *The Joseph Smith Hypocephalus*, 4).

10. Wepwawet, the "Opener of the Ways," identified with Osiris (Nibley, *The Message of the Joseph Smith Papyri*, 188–89).

11. Ra as creator, a composite god with Osiris (Wilkinson, *The Complete Gods and Goddesses of Ancient Egypt*, 35).

12. Min-Horus. Osiris is manifested in Min or "god of the lifted-arm." (Budge, *Osiris and the Egyptian Resurrection*, 1:21). (Note: There are at least twelve references to Osiris and his doctrine in this one document.)

Facsimile No. 3

The third facsimile is without question a document of Osiris.

Osiris

Osiris as a glorified being is sitting on his throne in the act of judgment upon an initiate who is on the way into his presence. We might ask the same

question with this document as we did with Facsimile No. 2: how thoroughly does this document relate to Osiris? To answer this question, we show a reconstruction wherein the hieroglyphs have been made distinct and translatable.

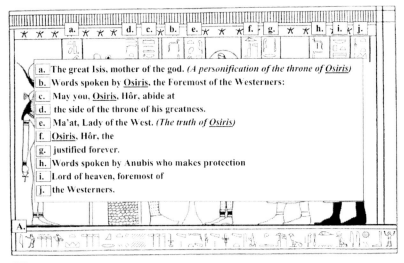

a. The great Isis, mother of the god. *(A personification of the throne of Osiris)*

b. Words spoken by Osiris, the Foremost of the Westerners:

c. May you, Osiris, Hôr, abide at

d. the side of the throne of his greatness.

e. Ma'at, Lady of the West. *(The truth of Osiris)*

f. Osiris, Hôr, the

g. justified forever.

h. Words spoken by Anubis who makes protection

i. Lord of heaven, foremost of

j. the Westerners.

A. The gods of the West, the gods of the cavern, the gods of the south, north, west, and east say: May Osiris, Hôr, justified, born of Taykhebyt, prosper.

(Note: The above transcription, transliteration, and translation of these figures was done by Dr. Michael D. Rhodes of BYU. They are used here with his permission. The reconstruction of the figures was done by the author.)

There are six references to Osiris and his doctrine in this document.

We started out this section asking these questions: Why would Abraham preserve such documents? What message do they contain that would make them valuable to him? And perhaps equally important: who were the Egyptians, and what were they doing that caused them to produce documents that would be of value to Abraham?

We have answered parts of these questions. We now know who the Egyptians were and why they produced such documents. We now need to see if we can discover why these documents would be valuable to Abraham, and why he would preserve them.

First of all, if these documents were used as "visual aids," they demonstrate the rather incredible imitation of the doctrine of Christ, and serve as witnesses to the antiquity of the Ancient Order that was imitated.

Second, they would serve as a ready-made platform for teaching the Egyptians the truth about Christ. We could imagine Abraham in his situation being somewhat like Paul, who said to the people, "For as I passed by, and beheld your devotions, I found an altar with this inscription, TO THE UNKNOWN GOD (in Abraham's case, TO THE MIGHTY GOD Osiris). Whom therefore ye ignorantly worship, him declare I unto you" (Acts 17:23).

Third, these documents of Egyptian origin lend themselves, like a template, to the telling of Abraham's own story.

Fourth, they are a witness that Abraham actually went into Egypt and are likely souvenirs of that experience, left as a legacy to his family—a witness that he actually did fulfill the commandment from God to teach the Egyptians.

How do we know that these documents were templates for the story of Abraham?

We wouldn't know that at all were it not for the Prophet Joseph Smith. Abraham tells us almost nothing about them. He makes a nominal reference to Facsimile No. 1 twice in his narrative, but everything else we know about them, we learn from the Prophet Joseph. And what is it we learn? Do we learn that they are imitations of the true and ancient order? No. Joseph could certainly have told us that. Do we learn that they can be used as a platform to teach the truth about Christ? No. Joseph could have told us that also. But he didn't. He only told us how the facsimiles can be used to tell Abraham's story. Knowing this, we can figure out the rest for ourselves based on Abraham's narrative and the battery of Egyptian material from that period that we have available in our day.

The Prophet Joseph provided the key to understanding the story of Abraham in the facsimiles. In major places in these documents where figures are identified as Osiris or relating to Osiris, the Prophet tells us that the figure represents Abraham. Now, Joseph is not telling us that Abraham is Osiris.

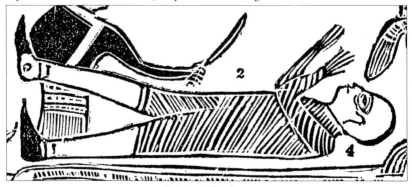

Osiris—Abraham
Facsimile No. 1, Figure 2

Left:
Osiris—Abraham
Facsimile No. 3, Figure 1

Right:
Osiris—Abraham
Facsimile No. 2, Figure 7

He is saying that Osiris represents a likeness of something that happened to Abraham. Whether we know it or not, that same key can be used if we want to see how Osiris relates to the Savior of whom he is an imitation. This key could even be used to see the results if we were to put ourselves in the place of Abraham.

So if these documents were to be used in Egypt, or even among Abraham's family, to tell his story, how are they used?

Facsimile No. 1

As a holder of the keys of the Priesthood of the Ancient Order, Abraham was sacrificed on an altar by the Egyptians. He was miraculously delivered through the ministering of an angel. This was in the likeness of Osiris, who was murdered by his brother, Set, and miraculously resurrected by the powers of the Horus Hawk.

After "escaping death on the altar," Abraham was said to have considered it an "equivalent of his own resurrection." (Nibley, "A New Look at the Pearl of Great Price," *Improvement Era,* April 1969, 71).

Facsimile No. 2

Having built an altar of sacrifice unto the Lord, Abraham saw God face-to-face. He was shown many of God's creations—the stars and planets—and he saw their relationships to the spirits or intelligences that God had fathered. During this great vision, he was commanded to teach these things to the Egyptians. The Holy Ghost ministered to him, and the grand key words of the Holy Priesthood were revealed to him as they had been revealed to Adam. He could have used the Hypocephalus of the Egyptians as a template to teach these things.

Facsimile No. 3

Abraham was invited by the pharaoh to sit on his own throne and teach his people. What a witness he could bear! He had been in the presence of God, seen him face-to-face, and viewed his creations. No wonder he is represented in a drawing as Osiris. What higher honor could the Egyptians pay him? He was as close to God as any mortal on earth, and his message would have resounded as the Lord says "as if from mine own mouth" (D&C 21:5).

As Abraham taught these things, it must certainly have taken on a dramatic air. Imagine him explaining to them that their belief in the God Osiris, who once dwelled on earth, had died and was resurrected, and from whom they traced their kingship and priesthood, was incorrect, for he [Abraham] had conversed face to face with Jesus Christ, and was commanded to teach them the truth. As taken aback as they must have been, these august Egyptian leaders seem to have kept the whole thing to themselves, for a public knowledge of it would have certainly destroyed their power and authority over the people. They kindly invited Abraham to leave the kingdom because there could not be two heads at one time (Nibley, "A New Look at the Pearl of Great Price," *Improvement Era,* May, 1969, 91, fn). And of course, significantly, no change or correction to their Osirian doctrine shows up in any of their public teachings.

So what was the purpose of Abraham's visit? To help answer that question, we will point out that six hundred years before Christ, Nephi was prompted to make a separate record of the spiritual events among his people. He did not know why he was asked to do it. Only that it was "for a wise purpose; for thus it whispereth me, according to the workings of the Spirit of the Lord which is in me" (Words of Mormon 1:7). We now know that the wise purpose was to correct a mistake made by a man more than twenty-five hundred years later.

If an all-wise creator would trigger an act that would have the effect of the correction of a man's mistake far, far away in the future, could we not imagine that the commandment of the Lord to Abraham to go down into Egypt was akin to that same thing, resulting in the Latter-day Saints having a Book of Abraham some thirty-three hundred years later? And not just a Book of Abraham, but three Egyptian documents containing a solemn witness of the antiquity of the doctrine of Christ through the mirror of Osiris, and a testimony of the mission of Abraham in Egypt.

Like the Book of Mormon, these things were preserved to come forth to us in our day. If that were not the case, they might have been discarded as worn-out visual aids. That they were carefully preserved by Abraham shows his feelings about them. That they were placed in our book of scripture by the Prophet Joseph Smith shows how he felt about them. When we acquire that same spirit, we will begin to appreciate their value.

CHAPTER 2

A Brief Overview of the Gods and Symbols of Egypt as Found in the Facsimiles

One of the blocks to beginning the study of Egyptian in our facsimiles is the presence of animal representations. We may think this strange indeed. But let's say a word about that.

When Adam was placed in the Garden of Eden, the Lord gave him an assignment to name the animals (see Genesis 2:19–20; Moses 3:19–20; Abraham 5:20–21). In addition, Adam was told that he was to "have dominion over . . . every living thing that moveth upon the earth" (Moses 2:28). Of these things the Lord said, "all things have their likeness, and all things are created and made to bear record of me, both things which are temporal, and things which are spiritual; things which are in the heavens above, and things which are on the earth, and things which are in the earth, and things which are under the earth, both above and beneath: all things bear record of me" (Moses 6:63).

Commenting on this, Joseph Smith said:

> After man was created, he was not left without intelligence

or understanding . . . God conversed with him face to face. In his presence he was permitted to stand, and from his own mouth he was permitted to receive instruction. He heard his voice, walked before him and gazed upon his glory, while intelligence burst upon his understanding, and enabled him to give names to the vast assemblage of his maker's works. . . . From the foregoing we learn man's situation at his first creation; the knowledge with which he was endowed, and the high and exalted station in which he was placed—lord, or governor of all things on the earth, and at the same time enjoying communion . . . with his maker, without a vail to separate between." (Smith, *Lectures on Faith,* 14–15)

It seems that the idea of Adam naming the animals takes on a greater significance than at first thought. His powers of discernment must have stretched wider than the garden, for in the same spirit in which he later "predicted whatsoever should befall his posterity unto the latest generation" (D&C 107:56), he must have seen and discerned what each animal was, had been, and would become in order to discover the truth of what it really was—and the manner in which it bore record or likeness of its creator.

Significantly, the scriptures note that "whatsoever Adam called every living creature, that was the name thereof" (Genesis 2:19), conveying that it was the name that God had called it in the first instance and that Adam was discovering it as part of being tutored in the eternal nature of things. The point of this seems to be that each animal in some majestic way mirrored some divine trait or characteristic of its creator. That being so, it becomes easier to see why such things as the bee might become the symbol of God's work and glory in the "hive" of His kingdom. The name *Deseret* as applied to the bee has come down to us from the Jaredites (see Ether 2:3), whose language was not changed at the tower of Babel (see Ether 1:35). From all our experience with the word *deseret* in this dispensation, it is easy to see how, in all probability, it derived from what bees are and what they do. Those functions were not observable by Adam in the garden for there was no reproduction there, hence the gift of revelation in the naming process.

It may be that the idea of animal symbolism was connected in some way with the pure Adamic language, so that the dove, for example, or the lamb always elicited the exalted view of the Holy Ghost and the Savior when they were used in a theological setting. The Prophet Joseph alluded to this when he said, "The sign of the dove was instituted before the creation of the world, a witness for the Holy Ghost, and the devil cannot come in the sign of a dove" (Smith, *Teachings,* 276).

If this exalted view of the animals came down from Adam as part of the heritage of the true and ancient order, it is no wonder that the Egyptians, and for that matter many other subsequent cultures, adopted it.

And the likening process was not limited to animals. "The peoples of the ancient Middle East loved imagery and figurative language and used them constantly. They saw spiritual parallels in the natural characteristics of things around them every day. They observed animals, objects, events, and actions, and then used those observations to express or teach figurative truths. In other words, the choice of symbols was not arbitrary or capricious; it was the nature of the item used that led to its use as a symbol. Therefore, if we take time to examine the symbols and ponder why the ancients chose them to represent symbolic truths, we often find important insights into their meaning" (Lund, *Selected Writings,* 68).

With that much of an introduction, we now turn our attention to the listing and identification of the Egyptian gods and representations that appear in the facsimiles. The animal heads on some of them actually figure in their representation of a particular aspect of god.

Facsimile No. 1

Figure 1		**The Horus Hawk** The Principle of ascension to the throne, symbol of divine kingship. The power of light over darkness (Hart, *Egyptian Gods and Goddesses,* 87; Budge, *The Gods of the Egyptians,* 1:475).
Figure 2		**Osiris** Rising off the altar of death at the command of Horus (Budge, *Osiris and the Egyptian Resurrection,* 2:2, 40).

Figure 3		**Anubis** The god of death and embalming. (Brodrick, *A Concise Dictionary*, 19)
Figure 4		**A Lion-couch** The bier from which Osiris arose from the dead (Budge, *Osiris and the Egyptian Resurrection*, 2:39; this source shows thirty examples of this lion-couch).
Figure 5–8		The Four Canopic gods Representing the four cardinal directions, and protection for the dead until the resurrection (Wilkinson, *The Complete Gods and Goddesses*, 88).
Figure 9		**The Crocodile** A symbol of death, seen as "the raging one," the "devourer of the dead," "great of death," and "the god of water." As "Sobek," he was associated with the Egyptian king and could act as a symbol of pharaonic might (Wilkinson, 218–19).
Figure 10		**The Lotus flower and Unguent Jar on Stand** A symbol of life springing from death, and the promise of inexhaustible life (Bonwick, *Egyptian Belief*, 243).
Figure 11		**The pillars of heaven** The doors of passage for the dead. It is always a passageway into another world, a sacred ceremonial gate of heaven or the underworld. *(5:September 1969:93–94)*

| Figure 12 | | **The heavens—great waters**
The "cosmic ocean," or the "vast domain of space" (Nibley, "A New Look," *Improvement Era,* October 1969, 87). |

Facsimile No. 2

Figure 1		**Khnum** The Ram-headed god of creation, representing the idea of "the most high" and the principle of virility (Wilkinson, *The Complete Gods and Goddesses,* 194).
Figure 2		**Amon-Ra** The creator god who, although "hidden," is manifest in the sun (Wilkinson, 92).
Figure 3		**Ra (Re)** The creator sun-god of Heliopolis, who permeates the three realms of the sky, earth and Underworld, who sails forth in a solar boat in his celestial journeys (Hart, *Egyptian Gods,* 179–82).
Figure 4		**Seker (Soker)** A hawk-headed god representing the "kingdom of death" *(26:55a,626b)* He is the personification of the emerging from the mummy bindings in the resurrection (Rhodes, *The Joseph Smith Hyposephalus,* 9–10).

Figure 5		**Hathor** The cow-headed goddess symbolized the idea of a mother who nourishes and nurtures, especially the king. She is the mother of Horus, "the substance of the sun" (Budge, *Osiris and the Egyptian Resurrection,* 2:57).
Figure 6		**The Four Sons of Horus** These gods represent the idea of the four cardinal directions of the earth, for example, people from all nations. They also represent the idea of protection and preservation (Budge, *Osiris,* 1:3, 40, 70–71, 327).
Figure 7		**Min-Horus** A composite god representing the virility of Min, and the kingship of Horus (Wilkinson, *The Complete Gods and Goddesses,* 115–16).
Figure 8		**The Ankh Symbol** This symbol is a knot or sash, representing the idea of binding as an "oath" or "covenant" (Nibley, *Lehi in the Desert,* 201).
Figure 18		**The Pupil of the Eye of Horus** Facsimile No. 2 is the pupil of the eye of Horus, the "resplendent end of the period of justification through which we shall pass in order to be admitted into the bosom of the supreme God" (Bonwick, *Egyptian Belief,* 210).

Figure 22–23		**The Apes of the dawn** The apes, due to their curious habit of holding up their hands to receive the first warming rays of the sun after the cold desert night as if worshiping the sun at its rising, are often found in connection with the sun (Rhodes, *The Joseph Smith Hypocephalus*, 8). They are forms of the two goddesses, Isis and Nephthys (Rossiter, *The Book of the Dead*, 36–37).

Facsimile No 3

Figure 1		**Osiris** The son of Ra, the god of life, suffering, death, and resurrection. The Judge of the dead (Budge, *The Gods of the Egyptians*, 2:141).
Figure 1a		**The *atef* crown of Osiris** The Atef crown, is the "the oldest and holiest of Pharaoh's many crowns. The two big feathers on it are emblems of spirit and truth, the symbols of Shu, the oldest and most 'spiritual' of the gods, and of Maat, who is truth itself" (Nibley, *Lehi in the Desert*, 336).
Figure 1b		**The Crook and Flail of Osiris** The "crook and flail" scepters held by Osiris designate "justice and judgment" and the office of "priesthood and kingship" (Nibley, *Abraham*, 142–43).

Figure 2		Isis The throne personified as the mother of the king (Hart, *Egyptian Gods*, 101).
Figure 3		The Lotus flower and Unguent Jar on Stand A symbol of life springing from death, and the promise of inexhaustible life (Bonwick, *Egyptian Belief*, 243).
Figure 4		Maat The symbol of truth, divine order, straightness, law, justice, and so forth (Budge, *The Gods of the Egyptians*, 1:417).
Figure 5		Shulem "One of the king's principle waiters" (Facsimile No. 3 explanations, Figure 5; see also Song of Solomon 6:13).
Figure 6		Anubis The keeper of the mysteries. The Jackal head represents the idea of a messenger going before to open the way (Gardiner, *Egyptian Grammar*, 459).
Facsimile 3		The Court of Osiris A representation of the courtroom, or throne-room, of the king, or the judgment hall of the god. It has a canopy of stars, and represents the majesty and power associated with the office of government (Budge, *Osiris and the Egyptian Resurrection*, 1:319).

Basic Principles Associated with the Egyptian Idea of God in the Facsimiles

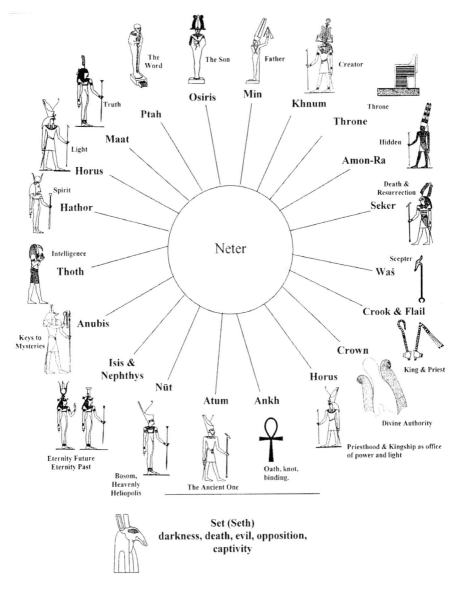

Ntr, pronounced neter, is the Egyptian name for God (Hornung, *Conceptions of God,* 33).

A Correlation with the Attributes of God in the Scriptures

Concepts of God in the Scriptures

1. God is a Father (see Acts 17:28; Moses 6:51; Hebrews 12:9).
2. God is a Creator (see Moses 3:4; Isaiah 64:8; Jeremiah 18:6).
3. God sits on a throne (see D&C 88:13).
4. God is hidden (see Job 34:29; Isaiah 8:17; 2 Nephi 18:17; Job 23:3, 8–9).
5. God is resurrected (D&C 130:22).
6. God holds a scepter (see D&C 106:6; Hebrews 1:8; Numbers 24:17).
7. God is a king and a priest (see Smith, *Teachings,* 346–47).
8. God wears a crown (see Facsimile 2, Figure 3; Isaiah 28:5).
9. God is the author of the priesthood, which is an office of power and light (see 1 Peter 2:5, 9; Abraham 1:18).

10. God is the author of the covenant, the sealing and binding power, and eternal life (see D&C 132:46; Mosiah 26:20; 3 Nephi 15:8–9).

11. God is the God of Adam, the Ancient of Days (Moses 6:51; D&C 27:11; D&C 138:38).

12. God is in the "bosom" of eternity, and with him is the Holy City of the New Jerusalem (see D&C 38:4; D&C 76:13, 39; D&C 88:13; Moses 7:30–31; Moses 7:47, 63, 69; Luke 16:22; Proverbs 5:20).

13. God is from "all eternity to all eternity" (see Moroni 8:18; D&C 39:1; Moses 6:67).

14. God is the "opener of the ways" and the holder and giver of keys or key words or "words of power" (see D&C 132:45; Isaiah 22:22; D&C 84:19; D&C 130:11; Facsimile No. 2, Explanation: Figures 2–3, 7; D&C 29:30; Moses 1:32; Moses 2:5; 1 Nephi 10:7–8; 1 Nephi 17:13; Matthew 11:10; Luke 1:76).

15. God is manifest by the Holy Ghost, who writes, records, bears witness, and seals (see D&C 124:4; D&C 76:53; Ephesians 4:30; Moses 6:61; Hebrews 10:15; D&C 1:39).

16. God, although a physical being, is a spirit (see John 4:24; D&C 84:45–46).

17. God is light (see 1 John 1:5; D&C 93:36; D&C 88:7–13).

18. God is a God of truth and order (see D&C 1:39; Ether 3:1; Abraham 4:18; Alma 13:16).

19. God is the "word" (see John 1:1; Alma 38:9; Revelation 19:13; Moroni 8:9).

20. God is manifested through His Son (see Moses 6:57; D&C 138:3; John 1:1; JST John 1:1; Hebrews 1:1–2).

21. God is called a lion (see Revelation 5:5; Hosea 11:10).

22. God is called a lamb, who is "Lord of lords, and King of kings" (see Revelation 17:14; 1 Nephi 11:21).

23. God is called "the mighty God" (see Isaiah 9:6; Psalm 50:1).

24. God has an arch-enemy, Satan (see D&C 86:3; D&C 19:3; D&C 76:28; Moses 1:13; D&C 29:36).

25. God's discernment and presence is sometimes referred to as his eye or eyes (see D&C 1:1; Revelation 4:6; Psalm 11:4; JST Psalm 11:4; Proverbs 20:8; Jeremiah 32:19; Psalm 32:8).

26. God is governor over the "four directions" (see 3 Nephi 20:13; Luke 13:29; Revelation 21:13; 2 Chronicles 4:4; Psalm 107:2–3; Zechariah 14:4; D&C 124:128).

PROLOGUE TO A STUDY
OF THE FACSIMILES

In the chapters that follow, we ask three questions about each facsimile and each figure therein:

1. What does this document or figure represent in the world of the Egyptians?
2. What meaning is given to this document or figure by either the Prophet Joseph Smith or Abraham?
3. If we look at this Egyptian figure as an imitation, what gospel principles can we see in it?

Once we have identified what the figure is in the world of the Egyptians and have looked at the meaning given to it by the Prophet Joseph Smith or Abraham, we ask: Why do they sometimes differ?

Joseph Smith and Abraham are not trying to explain the meaning of the Egyptian figures. Joseph Smith is explaining how Abraham used the Egyptian documents and figures as a template to tell his own story. In other words, the Egyptian documents and figures serve as a template.

We could compare it to using the principles of the story of Little Red Riding Hood to tell your own story. Part 1: Little Red Riding Hood goes to her grandmother's house. Part 2: Her grandmother tells her not to talk to the big bad wolf. Part 3: She meets up with the big bad wolf in disguise, and so forth. So you tell your story using the template of her story. However, in your case, you might visit your Aunt Nellie, so the grandmother becomes your aunt. And maybe your aunt tells you not to accept rides from strangers. Shortly afterwards, you meet up with a friend, who is actually a stranger in disguise.

We can certainly understand that in putting your aunt in the position of the grandmother, you are not trying to tell us that the grandmother is your aunt but that the grandmother's position in the story is the same as that of your aunt. It is the same with the wolf.

In this likeness, each of the facsimiles are Egyptian templates, or prototypes or models, which Abraham uses to tell his story. The figures have their own meaning, but in this case, Abraham is using them to say something else. His story does not explain the Egyptian figures any more than your Aunt Nellie explains Little Red Riding Hood's grandmother.

This is the same principle as likening the scriptures unto ourselves. How often we have heard the admonition to "put our own name in the verses." The story of Nephi becomes a template or a prototype by which we can relate our own experience. Certainly, no one is expected to believe that while we are comparing our own experience to that of Nephi, we are identifying and defining his experience. When the story is over, Nephi is still Nephi and we are still ourselves.

This helps us understand why the meanings of the facsimiles in relationship to Abraham are different than the meanings understood by the Egyptologists.

So, what do we do with the Egyptian meanings? Joseph invites us to go to work on them. He says in effect, "if you can find out these numbers, so let it be," and "they will be given in the own due time of the Lord" (explanation to Facsimile 2). This is a challenge to seek revelation for ourselves and learn how the Egyptians imitated the true and ancient order, and recorded some of their most intimate and sacred doctrines in these facsimiles. If we do this, we might discover the meanings of the "writings that cannot be revealed unto the world, but (are) to be had in the Holy Temple of God" (explanation to Facsimile 2, figure 8), and perhaps we could discover what other gospel principles all these incredible figures relate with.

CHAPTER 3

Facsímíle No. 1

Abraham on the Altar

What would a document of this nature represent in the world of the Egyptians?

- This document is a fairly typical representation of the death and resurrection of Osiris.
- It also represents the ceremony of a Sed-festival in which the Egyptian king, through a substitute, was ritually put to death and resurrected to renew his powers on the throne (Nibley, "A New Look at the Pearl of Great Price," *Improvement Era*, June 1969, 126).

What meaning is given to this document by the Prophet Joseph Smith or Abraham?

- Abraham was taken by the wicked priest of Pharaoh and placed on an altar to be sacrificed. The sacrifice was to be conducted "after

a.

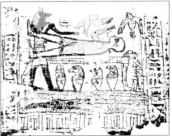

b.   *c.*

Above: (a) Facsimile No. 1 as found in the scriptures; (b) Facsimile No. 1 as found in the original Egyptian papyri (Hugh Nibley, "Background for the Church Historian's Fragment," *Improvement Era,* February 1968, 40); (c) A proposed restoration of the damaged areas, by Edward Ashment (Ashment, *The Facsimiles,* 39).

the manner of the Egyptians" (Abraham 1:11), which included all their rites and ceremonies. He was offered up because he was a faithful "High Priest, holding the right belonging to the fathers" (Abraham 1:2) who preached the gospel to the wicked people of his time. The pharaoh, by offering him as a substitute sacrifice, thought to ceremonially obtain his powers (Nibley, "A New Look at the Pearl of Great Price," *Improvement Era,* June 1969, 128), the greatest of which would be his priesthood.

If we look at this Egyptian document as an imitation, what gospel principles can we see in it?

- The figure on the altar can representt the death and resurrection of Christ.
- The act of sacrifice can represent the symbolic death and resurrection of baptism that each must go through to become like Christ. The four canopic gods can represent that principle is universal and applies to all men on the earth.
- The principle of opposition in all things.
- The hawk figure can represent the hope of deliverance from evil through faith in Christ and through His ordinances.

Figure 1

What does this figure represent in the world of the Egyptians?

- This is the Horus-hawk. In Egyptian mythology, birds are often used to represent the human spirit, not because human spirits look like birds but because the idea of a bird best represents the spirit's lightness and its ability to move freely and spurn the heavy gravity of the earth (Nibley, "A New Look at the Pearl of Great Price," *Improvement Era,* July 1969, 109).
- The Horus-hawk represents any god or messenger coming to the aid or assistance of the faithful in distress. It is the principle of light overcoming darkness and deliverance from the powers of evil. It can refer to the power of god coming down or a person's own spirit returning to the body during the resurrection (Nibley, "A New Look at the Pearl of Great Price," *Improvement Era,* May 1969, 90; July 1969, 109–10).

- The idea of Horus relates to the strength of the reigning king, the concept of divine kingship, and protection against Seth, or the god of evil (Hart, *A Dictionary of Egyptian Gods and Goddesses*, 87, 93).
- One source says, "Thy brow is under the protection of Anpu, and thy head and face, O beautiful one, are before the holy Hawk" (Budge, *The Book of the Dead*, 630).

What meaning is given to this figure by the Prophet Joseph Smith or Abraham?

- "The Angel of the Lord" (Explanation: Figure 1).
- Abraham explains that "the angel of (the Lord's) presence stood by me, and immediately unloosed my bands" (Abraham 1:15). "The Lord broke down the altar of Elkenah, and of the gods of the land, and utterly destroyed them, and smote the priest that he died" (Abraham 1:20). In speaking with the Lord later, Abraham affirms that "thou didst send thine angel to deliver me from the gods of Elkenah" (Abraham 2:13). And finally, the Lord himself affirms, "The Lord thy God sent his angel to deliver thee from the hands of the priest of Elkenah" (Abraham 3:20).

If we look at this Egyptian figure as an imitation, what gospel principles can we see in it?

- The Spirit of the Lord.
- The power of the Holy Ghost.
- The ministering of angels—an angel flying through the midst of heaven.
- The spirit and body being joined together in the resurrection.
- The idea of ascension (see Moses 7:59; John 20:17; Psalm 24:3).
- The idea of "mount[ing] up . . . as upon eagles' wings" (D&C 124:99; Isaiah 40:31).
- Christ will "rise from the dead, with healing in his wings" (2 Nephi 25:13).
- "Their eyes are a representation of light and knowledge, that is, they are full of knowledge; and their wings are a representation of power, to move, to act, etc." (D&C 77:4).

Figure 2

(Budge, *Osiris and the Egyptian Resurrection,* 2:45)

What does this figure represent in the world of the Egyptians?

- Osiris, who has been put to death by his brother Set, is rising from the dead (see Brodrick, *A Concise Dictionary of Egyptian Archaeology,* 120–21; Griffiths, *The Origins of Osiris and His Cult,* 8–9, 14–15).
- He rises from the lion couch by the command of Horus (Budge, *Osiris and the Egyptian Resurrection,* 2:40); Horus is the messenger who comes to deliver Osiris from the dead.
- In the formal symbolism of Egypt, this figure is represented as being in the attitude of prayer, "right foot forward, hands raised before the face" (Nibley, "A New Look at the Pearl of Great Price," *Improvement Era,* December 1968, 31).

What meaning is given to this figure by the Prophet Joseph Smith or Abraham?

- "Abraham fastened up on an altar" (Explanation: Figure 2).
- "And as they lifted up their hands upon me, that they might offer me up and take away my life, behold, I lifted up my voice unto the Lord my God, and the Lord hearkened and heard, and he filled me with the vision of the Almighty, and the angel of his presence stood by me, and immediately unloosed my bands" (Abraham 1:15).

If we look at this Egyptian figure as an imitation, what gospel principles can we see in it?

- New birth arising out of a former death; overcoming opposition; repentance and forgiveness; baptism; resurrection, and so forth (Mosiah 15:23; D&C 29:43).

- The necessity of asking God for help in our struggles, and the witness that He hears and answers our prayers (Alma 36:27).
- It is significant that of all the altar victims seen in these kinds of documents, only Abraham is clothed. As clothing would certainly interfere with ritual sacrifice, the Egyptians either did not want it removed or they could not remove it. Since it appears more like underclothing rather than outer clothing, it may have been his "garment of the holy priesthood" (Asay, "The Temple Garment: An Outward Expression of an Inward Commitment," *Ensign,* August 1997, 18–23), which the faithful are promised is "a shield and a protection" as long as covenants are kept (Packer, *The Holy Temple,* 75, 79).

Figure 3

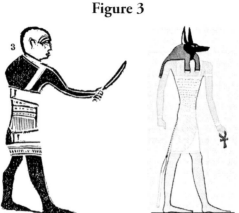

(Budge, *The Gods of the Egyptians,* 2:431)

What does this figure represent in the world of the Egyptians?

- This figure is normally a priest in the regalia of Anubis with a jackal-head mask. He is the "god of burials" with the idea of "springing to life" thereafter. He is the embalmer of the dead and the guide who leads the dead toward the throne of Osiris (Hart, *A Dictionary of Egyptian Gods and Goddesses,* 22–25).
- One of the names of Anubis was Ap-uat or Wepwawet. Wepwawet means literally "the opener of the ways." His office was to introduce the souls of the departed into the "divine hidden land." He holds the Ankh, a symbol of (eternal) life (Brodrick, *A Concise Dictionary of Egyptian Archaeology,* 14, 19, 23).

What meaning is given to this figure by the Prophet Joseph Smith or Abraham?

- ♦ "The idolatrous priest of Elkenah (a priest of Pharaoh) attempting to offer up Abraham as a sacrifice" (Explanation: Figure 3).
- "My fathers . . . endeavored to take away my life by the hand of the priest of Elkenah. The priest of Elkenah was also the priest of Pharaoh" (Abraham 1:5, 7).

If we look at this Egyptian figure as an imitation, what gospel principles can we see in it?

- The priest or elder who lays a candidate under the waters of baptism is, in effect, performing a ritual death and resurrection. He, through the authority he holds, opens the way for the person to obtain eternal life and become like Christ.
- The idea of a priest "opening the way" relates to John the Baptist, who as an Elias opened the way for the Savior, both in his day and in our day, for the gospel to come forth.

Figure 4

(Budge, *Osiris and the Egyptian Resurrection,* 2:35)

What does this figure represent in the world of the Egyptians?

- The lion couch represented death. Certainly, anyone facing a lion faces sure death. But death is not the end. Death can be friendly and acts in the capacity of a conveyor. Death conveys a person toward eternal life. The tail of the lion is part of the key to its meaning, it is raised like the tail of a happy puppy. It is the signal that though there is serious business going on (death), continued life will come (Nibley, "A New Look at the Pearl of Great Price," *Improvement Era,* July 1969, 102–4).

What meaning is given to this figure by the Prophet Joseph Smith or Abraham?

- "The altar for sacrifice by the idolatrous priests, standing before the gods of Elkenah, Libnah, Mahmackrah, Korash, and Pharaoh" (Explanation: Figure 4).

• Abraham says that the priests were "offer[ing] up . . . [their] children" on this altar, and it was their custom to offer up "men, women, and children." The priest offered up on this altar a "thank-offering of a child" and "three virgins at one time . . . because of their virtue" (Abraham 1:8, 10, 11).

If we look at this Egyptian figure as an imitation, what gospel principles can we see in it?

• The lion-couch might represent a baptismal font, where one enters into a symbolic death and resurrection. This might be likened to entering into the mouth of a lion, and being delivered out of it, in the principle of resurrection.

• Death is "the merciful plan" of the great creator (2 Nephi 9:6); to do away with it "would destroy the great plan of happiness" (Alma 42:8).

• All are required to sacrifice. Some, like the three virgins, are required to sacrifice unto death. Examples of this type of sacrifice include Jesus Christ, John the Baptist, Abinadi, the women and children at the time of Alma and Amulek, and Joseph and Hyrum Smith.

Figures 5–8

(Rawlinson, *History of Ancient Egypt,* 1:397)

What do these figures represent in the world of the Egyptians?

• These gods were associated with the four cardinal directions. The human-headed Imsety represented the South, the jackal-headed Duamutef represents the East, the baboon-head Hapy represents the North, and the falcon-headed Qebesenuef represents the West. They are referred to as the sons of Horus or Osiris because they assist the deceased in ascending into the sky into the presence of Osiris. Likenesses of their heads were often carved on canopic jars in which the internal organs of the deceased were preserved (see Wilkinson, *The Complete Gods and Goddesses of Ancient Egypt*, 88; Brodrick, *A Concise Dictionary of Egyptian Archaeology*, 38). Canopic may refer to the canopy of heaven of which these gods were the four corners.

- Because the Egyptians emphasized the fourfold nature of all things, their ceremonies were often repeated four times. Because this was hard to depict in drawings, they drew the four canopic gods to represent that it was to be repeated four times, once to each of the cardinal directions (Nibley, "A New Look at the Pearl of Great Price," *Improvement Era*, July 1969, 104).

- One of the missions of these four gods was to watch over the "dust" of the body of the deceased, which was thought to be scattered over the whole world and had to be brought back together again before its resurrection could be accomplished. They also represented the four elements taken from those four quarters to make up the body of man in the first place. They represent both the dissolution and scattering of the elements of the body, and then the gathering in of those parts and elements for the resurrection (Nibley, "A New Look at the Pearl of Great Price," *Improvement Era*, July 1969, 103).

What meaning is given to this figure by the Prophet Joseph Smith or Abraham?

- Figure 5. "The idolatrous god of Elkenah."
- Figure 6. "The idolatrous god of Libnah."
- Figure 7. "The idolatrous god of Mahmackrah."
- Figure 8. "The idolatrous god of Korash" (Explanation: Figures 5–8).
- In his description of these gods, Abraham refers to them as "the gods of Elkenah, Libnah, Mahmackrah, Korash, and also a god like unto that of Pharaoh, king of Egypt" (Abraham 1:13). Notice that he does not say "the god Elkenah, the god Libnah" and so forth, for as Nibley points out, these were gods over peoples and the names were the names of those peoples—people who had gathered to participate in these ceremonies from the four directions of the earth (Nibley, "A New Look at the Pearl of Great Price," *Improvement Era*, August 1969, 82). Significantly, Abraham says, "the Lord broke down the altar of Elkenah, and of the gods of the

land, and utterly destroyed them" (Abraham 1:20).

- In keeping with the idea that many of the ceremonies of the Egyptians were repeated four times, Abraham says, "this priest had offered upon this altar three virgins at one time" (Abraham 1:11) and "the priests laid violence upon me, that they might slay me also, as they did those virgins" (Abraham 1:12), signifying that he was the fourth to be offered.

- One of the purposes of repeating the ceremonies four times was to honor and recognize the people from the directions from which they had come. This signified the Egyptian belief that their ceremonies would benefit all. The offering of sacrifices to the four gods symbolized the planned resurrection of all things in all directions under heaven.

- In the true spirit of the four directions, Abraham was given a promise: "And thy seed shall be as the dust of the earth, and thou shalt spread abroad to the west, and to the east, and to the north, and to the south: and in thee and in thy seed shall all the families of the earth be blessed" (Genesis 28:14).

If we look at this Egyptian figure as an imitation, what gospel principles can we see in it?

- The scriptures speak of man coming from the dust in birth and returning to the dust in death (see Moses 4:25). King Benjamin spoke of his death as being "about to yield up this mortal frame to its mother earth" (Mosiah 2:26). The Lord said that "the grave must deliver up its captive bodies, and the bodies and the spirits of men will be restored one to the other; and it is by the power of the resurrection of the Holy One of Israel" (2 Nephi 9:12). Isaiah said, "Thy dead men shall live, together with my dead body shall they arise. Awake and sing, ye that dwell in dust . . . and the earth shall cast out the dead" (Isaiah 26:19). Reference to the earth yielding up the dead relates to the idea that the dead will come from all four directions. The Savior spoke of the gathering in these terms, "and they shall come from the east, and from the west, and from the north, and from the south, and shall sit down in the kingdom of God" (Luke 13:29).

- We see a fourfold nature in many of our teachings, for example, the placement of the oxen in our temples in the four cardinal directions; the idea of missionary work to the whole world; and the gathering in of all the dispersed of Israel.

- If these Egyptian gods relate to a heavenly canopy of which they are the four pillars, we can see an interesting likeness as the following scripture speaks of God, who is over all things, the heaven, the earth, the seas, and the kingdom of darkness, being asked to lift the great tent or canopy that hides Him from His creations and show Himself as He really is, that great being who presides over all the dimensions of eternity. "O Lord God Almighty, maker of heaven, earth, and seas, and of all things that in them are, and who controllest and subjectest the devil, and the dark and benighted dominion of Sheol—stretch forth thy hand; let thine eye pierce; let thy pavilion be taken up; let thy hiding place no longer be covered; let thine ear be inclined; let thine heart be softened, and thy bowels moved with compassion toward us" (D&C 121:4).

Figure 9

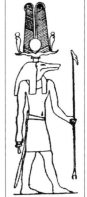

Above: La Farge, *Museums of Egypt,* 64; right: Brodrick, *A Concise Dictionary,* 15

What does this figure represent in the world of the Egyptians?

- The sacrifice on the altar was for the benefit of the king. He wanted to renew his powers on the throne, and to do that he believed that the flesh and blood of a sacrificial victim could be ceremonially transferred to him. In this case, it was particularly important to him that Abraham held the priesthood, for he hoped that through this process, he could become an heir to that as well. The crocodile was the means of doing that (Nibley, "A New Look at the Pearl of Great Price," *Improvement Era,* July 1969, 106–7).

• To understand the crocodile, we must go back to the foundations of Egyptian history, where newcomers to the land first discovered to their horror that it was already inhabited—by crocodiles. This was a fearful yet awesome thing, and the pharaohs, in order to dwell in the land, had to appease these animals. We note that they had no disposition to dispose of them, for they believed in the sanctity of life and that the crocodiles had as much right to be there as they did. In simple terms, the pharaoh had come across something greater than himself which had to be dealt with, and because appeasement is a form veneration, we see the crocodile rise in importance in the symbolism of Egypt and, at one time or another, portrayed with all the crowns of royalty, truly the 'god of pharaoh'. What is more, many pharaohs recognizing the awesome power residing in the crocodile, associated themselves with this beast, expressing their own power in terms of his, sometimes even dressing as a crocodile (Nibley, "A New Look at the Pearl of Great Price," *Improvement Era,* July 1969, 105–6). Some actually even called themselves by his name—Sobek (Budge, *The Book of the Kings of Egypt,* 1:81; at least nineteen pharaohs had Sobek as a part of their name).

• The Egyptians included the crocodile in their sacrificial ceremonies because they believed that if they gave some of the vital parts of the victim they were sacrificing to him, that he would ceremonially transform them into a rebirth for the king on the throne (Nibley, "A New Look at the Pearl of Great Price," *Improvement Era,* July 1969, 106–7).

What meaning is given to this figure by the Prophet Joseph Smith or Abraham?

• "The idolatrous god of Pharaoh" (Explanation: Figure 9).

• When Abraham was delivered from the Egyptians, "the Lord broke down the altar . . . and smote the priest that he died," which brought "great mourning in Chaldea and also in the court of Pharaoh" (Abraham 1:20). Why all the mourning? What had happened? Was the pharaoh sad because his priest was dead? No, it was because his great expectation of a regeneration and possibly even obtaining the priesthood was forever dashed. And because the people of his kingdom revered him, they mourned with him.

If we look at this Egyptian figure as an imitation, what gospel principles can we see in it?

- It is significant that the crocodile is in the water, for it is in the waters of baptism that a transformation takes place in the baptismal candidate as his sins are washed away. But in the Egyptian ceremony, the victim's vital parts were expended for the king and not for himself. However, if we remember, the Savior was also baptized in water, and because He had no sin, His baptism opened the way for Him to fulfilled all righteousness in transmitting the forgiveness of sins to all who would likewise be baptized in His name. Hence, the baptismal candidate is both a sacrificial victim and a renewed being, for he rises up regenerated by the flesh and blood of Christ, in just the manner that the Egyptian king had hoped to be.

Figure 10

(Patrick, *All Colour Book,* 36)

What does this figure represent in the world of the Egyptians?

- It is an offering table covered with lotus flowers (Nibley, "A New Look at the Pearl of Great Price," *Improvement Era,* September 1969, 89). This symbol, in addition to appearing here, appears in both Facsimile No. 2 and Facsimile No. 3, and for the same reason. Joseph Smith gives the identical interpretation to them in Facsimile 1 and 3—Abraham in Egypt.
- While this figure appears with regularity in throne scenes such

Figure 2: Facsimile 2   Figure 3: Facsimile 2   Figure 3: Facsimile 3

as Facsimile No. 3, this is the only known instance in which it appears in a lion-couch scene (Nibley, "A New Look at the Pearl of Great Price," *Improvement Era,* September 1969, 90). To understand why it might be there, we first need to understand that the lotus expresses the basic idea of the theology of Osiris and is an emblem par excellence of Egyptian religion (ibid.). Entry into a new life and a continuation of life after death was tied up in the dead identifying himself with everything in which the principle of resurrection dwells—the morning star, the lotus, or the divine power of Atum. Its essence is the claim that the dead person is identical with Osiris who himself achieved this end (Griffiths, *The Origins of Osiris and His Cult,* 68).

- The lotus, or water lily, which grows in the swamps and marshy areas of Egypt, has peculiar characteristics. They "shut their flowers at eventide and retreat so far into the water that they cannot be reached by hand. At daybreak, oriented to the east, they strive upward again and open in the light" (Lurker, *The Gods and Symbols of Ancient Egypt,* 77).

- One writer who explained flowers that act in this manner said, "Picture a radar dish sitting in the middle of a . . . field, tracking a satellite, collecting, focusing, and concentrating radio signals to the very centre of the dish. Now look at the broad open blossom of the (lily) and imagine it as a sun dish, tracking the sun from horizon to horizon, focusing and collecting the heat rays in the very centre of the flower" (Bush, *Compact Guide to Wildflowers of the Rockies,* 99).

- The lotus rose with the flood and opened to the sun. The secret of this symbol lay in its productive powers. "The orifice of the cells being too small to let the seeds drop out when ripe, they shoot forth into new plants . . . the bulb of the vessel serving as a matrix to nourish them, until they acquire such a degree of magnitude as to break open, and release themselves. After which, like other aquatic plants, they take root wherever the current deposits them." The lotus is the "birthplace," "new birth," "inexhaustible life" (Bonwick, *Egyptian Belief and Modern Thought*, 243).

- The lotus holds the secret of life springing up spontaneously. The seed of life slept in the lotus. "All life finds earnest [hope] of the resurrection in the miracle of the lotus. The king is described in the Pyramid Texts as being 'in the lotus' at the moment he awakes from the sleep of death (Nibley, "A New Look at the Pearl of Great Price," *Improvement Era*, September 1969, 90–92). A wooden and painted portrait head of Tutankhamun from his tomb shows the king rising from a lotus blossom (Lurker, *The Gods and Symbols of Ancient Egypt*, 78).

(Gilbert, *Treasures*, color plate 1)

- Because of its symbolism, the lotus was used by both king as "host" and subject as "guest," to represent the protector and that which is being protected (Nibley, "A New Look at the Pearl of Great Price," *Improvement Era*, September 1969, 90–92).

- The lotus is the symbol of the land of Egypt and the embodiment of Pharaoh as the ruling power of Egypt, a beneficent and hospitable power. The lotus is most at home in situations of hospitality, where it represents both guest and host. In both capacities it can represent individuals, including foreigners in Egypt. The lotus is a sort of ticket. Every guest brings a token for his host and receives one in return, a sign of submission and love. The lotus marks the trail of the righteous man, the messenger of truth, bearing his light into dark and dangerous places (Nibley, "A New Look at the Pearl of Great Price," *Improvement Era*, September 1969, 92–93). For someone to have this personal insignia of the king on his own document would indicate that he had once been in the king's court and honored by him.

- The little spouted jug on the tall stand is an ointment jar for the use of honored guests (Nibley, "A New Look at the Pearl of Great Price," *Improvement Era,* September 1969, 93).

What meaning is given to this figure by the Prophet Joseph Smith or Abraham?

- According to Joseph Smith, the lotus in Figure 10 represents two entities and specifies their relationship. It is Abraham in Egypt, Abraham as guest, and Egypt as host. The lotus functioning here as a "stamp of official protection and safe conduct (a sort of visa as it were)" (Nibley, "A New Look at the Pearl of Great Price," *Improvement Era,* September 1969, 93).
- Abraham is the archetype of the righteous man, the bearer of revelation and preacher of righteousness, the courageous stranger in alien and hostile countries and courts (Nibley, "A New Look at the Pearl of Great Price," *Improvement Era,* September 1969, 93).
- Abraham, speaking the language of the Egyptians and understanding its symbolism, tells us that he was one, "having been myself a follower of righteousness, desiring also to be one who possessed great knowledge, and to be a greater follower of righteousness" (Abraham 1:2).
- The presentation table, with its lotus flower and ointment jar, shows that the person who is on the altar in Facsimile No. 1 is the same person who sits on the throne in Facsimile No. 3. It bears witness that Abraham has, in fact, been in the court of Pharaoh and been treated as an honored guest, that he is the preacher of righteousness, and that his message is the message symbolized by the lotus. Notice that, in both instances, the lotus flower is facing him, for he was the light sent by God to teach the Egyptians and in whom the message of life dwelt. If they would follow him as he was a follower of the Son of God, they could have eternal life. So can we!

If we look at this Egyptian figure as an imitation, what gospel principles can we see in it?

- Speaking of Israel, the Lord said, "I will be as the dew unto Israel: he shall grow as the *lily,* and cast forth his roots as Lebanon" (Hosea 14:5; emphasis added). This is surely a forecast that his people will finally one day *"follow him."* Nephi said, "I know that if ye shall *follow the Son,* with full purpose of heart . . . witnessing unto the

Father that ye are willing to take upon you the name of Christ, by baptism—yea, by *following your Lord and your Savior down into the water*, according to his word, behold, then shall ye receive the Holy Ghost; yea, then cometh the baptism of fire and of the Holy Ghost; and then can ye speak with the tongue of angels, and shout praises unto the Holy One of Israel" (2 Nephi 31:13; emphasis added).

"And then shall ye *immerse them in the water, and come forth again out of the water"* (3 Nephi 11:26; emphasis added). "Therefore we are buried with him by baptism *unto death:* that like as Christ was *raised up from the dead by the glory of the Father,* even so we also should *walk in newness of life"* (Romans 6:4; emphasis added).

"The ordinance of baptism by water, to be immersed therein in order to answer to the likeness of the dead, that one principle might accord with the other; to be immersed in the water and come forth out of the water is in the likeness of the resurrection of the dead in coming forth out of their graves; hence, this ordinance was instituted to form a relationship with the ordinance of baptism for the dead, being in likeness of the dead" (D&C 128:12). "Herein," said Joseph, "is glory and honor, and immortality and eternal life" (ibid.). "Then shall the righteous *shine forth as the sun* in the kingdom of their Father" (Matthew 13:43; emphasis added).

- The Gods are planters. "And the Gods planted a garden, eastward in Eden" (Abraham 5:8). "And I, the Lord God, planted the tree of life also in the midst of the garden, and also the tree of knowledge of good and evil" (Moses 3:9), and His faithful servants are "those whom I have set to be as plants of renown" (D&C 124:61), whose privilege it is to "follow the Son, with full purpose of heart" (2 Nephi 31:13). "Plant this word in your hearts" (Alma 33:23), and "we will compare the word unto a seed. Now, if ye give place,

(Nibley, "Background of the Church Historian's Fragment," *Improvement Era*, February 1968, 40)

Erman, *Life in Ancient Egypt,* 171

that a seed may be planted in your heart" (Alma 32:28). The lotus flower in its symbolism is a likeness of all these things.

- The lotus (lily) was "one of the principle ornaments of Solomon's temple" (1 Kings 7:19, 22, 26).

Figure 11

What does this figure represent in the world of the Egyptians?

- This figure represents a series of gates or pylons placed at the entrance to palaces or tombs, and while they may be placed there for decoration, one thing is known for sure, the central panel is always a door. This design was also repeated on the sides of wooden coffins, where we find the same vertical lines with empty spaces in between, designated as pillars with false doors between them. It is not hard to reach a conclusion that the false door on funerary object must represent "a passage for the dead" (Nibley, "A New Look at the Pearl of Great Price," *Improvement Era,* September 1969, 93). Special significance comes into play when we learn that this phenomena was also employed in Egyptian temples. There, it is always a passageway into the heaven or the underworld.

  The pillars make the gates, and there are references to the four pillars of heaven, which are sometimes represented with one, two, four, and even many more. Indeed, the ceiling of an Egyptian temple represents the sky and the columns supporting it, no matter how many, stand for the pillars of heaven. In drawings, the number of pillars seem to be determined by the space available to the artist scribe (Nibley, "A New Look at the Pearl of Great Price," Improvement Era, September 1969, 94).
- The sons of Horus were guardians of the pillars, which formed the four cardinal points. The four gods held the pillars of heaven and earth in position as gods of the four cardinal points "who embrace the four Pure Lands" and are devoted to the service of Osiris (Harris, "The Book of Abraham Facsimilies," 259).
- More recently the temple gate has come to be understood as the gate by which the Horus-hawk passes between earth and heaven, and by which the spirits pass between worlds above and below. "This communication was one of the great preoccupations of the Egyptian. The [gateway] was the instrument of this communica-

tion" (Nibley, "A New Look at the Pearl of Great Price," *Improvement Era,* October 1969, 85).

What meaning is given to this figure by the Prophet Joseph Smith or Abraham?

- The Prophet Joseph says that this figure is "designed to represent the pillars of heaven, as understood by the Egyptians" (Explanation: Figure 11).
- As Dr. Nibley points out, "It is full of quite unique features such as the crocodile, the pillars of heaven, . . . peculiar aspects of the human figures, the lotus stand, etc., all of which imply (without necessarily proving) the presentation of a special dramatic situation; peculiarities of the drawing supply further evidence that the artist was trying to tell a particular story" (Nibley, *Abraham in Egypt,* 44–45).

If we look at this Egyptian figure as an imitation, what gospel principles can we see in it?

- Speaking of the Lord, the prophet Job said, "The pillars of heaven tremble and are astonished at his reproof" (Job 26:11).
- The great columns, "the Pillars of Jachin and Boaz," of Solomon's temple have been thought to represent the "pillars of heaven" (Madsen, *The Temple in Antiquity,* 147). "The sun was thought to have risen between the columns of the two lotus-crowned pillars, Boaz and Jakin, that flanked the main entrance to Solomon's temple, at the Equinoxes" (Nibley, "A New Look at the Pearl of Great Price," *Improvement Era,* October 1969, 86).
- The place where the heavens are observed is the place where they are closest to the earth, where heaven and earth touch; the stone pillars of the shrine are the pillars and ladders of heaven (see Nibley, *The Message of the Joseph Smith Papyri,* 152). This brings to mind the dream of Jacob wherein he saw "a ladder set up on the earth, and the top of it reached to heaven: and behold the angels of God ascending and descending on it" (Genesis 28:12). "And Jacob rose up early in the morning, and took the stone that he had put for his pillows, and set it up for a *pillar,* and poured oil upon the top of it. And he called the name of that place Beth-el. . . . And this stone, which I have set for a *pillar,* shall be *God's house*" (Genesis 28:18,

19, 22; emphasis added).
- The central gate suggests the straight and narrow way, or path, that leads to eternal life. In his discussion of this point, Nephi ties all these things together for us. "O then, my beloved brethren, come unto the Lord, the Holy One. Remember that his *paths* are righteous. Behold, the *way* for man is narrow, but it lieth in a straight

(Nibley, "Background of the Church Historian's Fragment," *Improvement Era*, February 1968, 40; Nibley, "A New Look," *Improvement Era*, February 68, 40)

course before him, and the keeper of the *gate* is the Holy One of Israel; and he employeth no servant there; and there is none other *way* save it be by the *gate;* for he cannot be deceived, for the Lord God is his name" (2 Nephi 9:41; emphasis added).

Figure 12

What does this figure represent in the world of the Egyptians?

- The hatched lines in this figure are an expanded representation of the Egyptian sign for water (Gardiner, *Egyptian Grammar,* 490). The representation of the crocodile (to the above right) shows the same zigzag pattern as our facsimile. The horizontal rows of hatchings in alternating directions are a common Egyptian way of showing big waters. On the Cenotaph of Seti 1st, they are used to depict the waters of the cosmic ocean (Nibley, "A New Look at the Pearl of Great Price," *Improvement Era,* October 1969, 87). The cosmic ocean represents the vast domain of space, and it is properly represented sitting over the symbols of the pillars of heaven (Figure 11) as they were thought to hold it up (Peterson, *The Pearl of Great Price,* 49).
- Because the artist-scribe was making a quick, freehand drawing, he

drew straight horizontal lines so that his zigzag water signs would be lined up. Those lines are not present in more precise and accurate drawings (Nibley, "A New Look at the Pearl of Great Price," *Improvement Era,* October 1969, 87–88).

- The "expanse or firmament over our heads" is exactly what these hatched horizontal strips were meant by the Egyptians to signify. The heavenly solar bark of Ra sailed in these cosmic waters (Budge, *Osiris and the Egyptian Resurrection,* 1:117, 163; this is depicted in Figure 3 of Facsimile No. 2). The gods go forth in their ships to plough and plant the earth. They also make their journey to the house of Horus in the firmament (Budge, *Osiris and the Egyptian Resurrection,* 2:334).

Because the Egyptians thought of heaven as a cosmic ocean that, if traversed, must be done by ship, we often find boats and models of boats buried with the kings. A whole book has been written

about a huge disassembled boat, buried and discovered beside the great pyramid of Cheops. It has now been taken out and assembled (Jenkins, *The Boat Beneath the Pyramid*). Even the throne of Ra was situated in a divine ship (Silverman, *Masterpieces of Tutankhamun,* 39; Facsimile 2:3).

What meaning is given to this figure by the Prophet Joseph Smith or Abraham?

- The Prophet Joseph says that this figure is called "Raukeeyang, signifying expanse, or the firmament over our heads; but in this case, in relation to this subject, the Egyptians meant it to signify Shaumau, to be high, or the heavens, answering to the Hebrew word, Shaumahyeem" (Explanation: Figure 12). The sense of this explanation is that the meaning of the figure is expanse or the firmament over our heads, but this is a special case, and the meaning here is "to be high, or the heavens . . . emphasizing their height and aloofness" (Nibley,

"A New Look at the Pearl of Great Price," *Improvement Era,* October 1969, 88). Notice Joseph says that the Egyptians have two words, Raukeeyang and Shaumau, that have approximate but different meanings. One has been chosen over the other, and the second word relates to the meaning of the Hebrew word, Shaumahyeem.

This tells us that for all its crudeness, this document has been carefully crafted to convey a specific message. Did Abraham, who knew the language of the Egyptians and what specific meaning to attach to a multilayered symbol so they could understand it, do the crafting? And is it Abraham, a Hebrew who draws the parallel of an Egyptian symbol to a Hebrew word, or is it Joseph Smith, an avid student of Hebrew, who does it? It seems unlikely that the Egyptians would have done so.

If Abraham is the artist, it would explain the reason why an everyday, ordinary Egyptian document contains the anomalies that perfectly fit his experience and why the Prophet Joseph would say Abraham is the main character in it. But there is more. The Egyptian word Raukeeyang also shows up in Facsimile No. 2, where it not only carries the same meaning as it does here but also relates to a "numerical figure, in Egyptian signifying one thousand; answering to the measuring of time" (Facsimile No. 2:4.) This links Facsimile Nos. 1 and 2 together in a curious way, showing that they must surely have the same author with the same emphasis and the same point of view.

If we look at this Egyptian figure as an imitation, what gospel principles can we see in it?

- ◆ We read in the scriptures of many things that relate to the firmament of heaven and to the vastness of space:
- • D&C 88:12: "Light proceedeth forth from the presence of God to fill the immensity of space."
- • D&C 88:37: "There is no space in the which there is no kingdom; and there is no kingdom in which there is no space."
- • Abraham 3:24: "We will go down, for there is space there, and we will take of these materials, and we will make an earth whereon these may dwell."
- • Moses 2:8: "I, God, called the firmament Heaven."
- • D&C 88:45: "The earth rolls upon her wings, and the sun giveth

his light by day, and the moon giveth her light by night, and the stars also give their light, as they roll upon their wings in their glory, in the midst of the power of God."

- D&C 76:70: "Whose glory is that of the sun, even the glory of God, the highest of all, whose glory the sun of the firmament is written of as being typical."
- Abraham 3:13: "And he said unto me: This is Shinehah, which is the sun. And he said unto me: Kokob, which is star. And he said unto me: Olea, which is the moon. And he said unto me: Kokaubeam, which signifies stars, or all the great lights, which were in the firmament of heaven."
- Psalm 68:4: "Sing unto God, sing praises to his name: extol him that rideth upon the heavens by his name JAH, and rejoice before him."
- Psalm 68:33: "To him that rideth upon the heavens of heavens, which were of old; lo, he doth send out his voice, and that a mighty voice."

The author of Facsimile No. 1 has given us a lot to think about. First of all, we see a man being sacrificed by the priest of Pharaoh. Notice the knife in the upper center of the drawing, exactly halfway between the eye of the priest and the eye of Abraham; it dominates the scene. We are being told that the man of God is being challenged by the world. Notice that the priest, the lion, and the crocodile all face the same direction—right. They are destroyers; they take life. They indicate the man on the couch is in grave danger. The remaining figures face left. They represent the power to save life. The four canopic gods have many meanings: four directions, the four elements of creation, and the fourfold nature of all the sacred ceremonies of the Egyptians. They are even shown as standing figures in Facsimile No. 2:6, where they are called "the four quarters of the earth." They were included in almost all scenes involving a new birth, a reviving, or a resurrection, for it is from the four directions that the dust of all the dead will be gathered unto life.

So we see the central rival figures, the prophet and the wicked priest who falsely claims the priesthood, are face to face. The author of this document is telling that story, but, says he, it is bigger than that. Abraham is God's representative; the priest, the representative of Satan. There is a universal and eternal conflict behind all this. So, he invites us to look through the center gate of the pillars of heaven, up through the cosmic ocean, through all space, yes, even into the very presence of God. There you will see things as they really are. There is opposition in all things. There always has been, and there always will be, and the inevitable reality is: righteousness always wins.

CHAPTER 4

Facsimile No. 2

Hypocephalus of Abraham

(Birch, *Proceedings,* 6:106)

The figure, above right, is a Hypocephalus much like Facsimile
No. 2. About one hundred of these have been found.

Facsimile 2

What would a document of this nature represent in the world of the Egyptians?

- Facsimile 2 belongs to a class of Egyptian religious documents called hypocephali, Greek for "under the head," a translation of the Egyptian *hr tp* with the same meaning. A hypocephalus is a small, disk-shaped object made of papyrus, stuccoed linen, bronze, gold, wood, or clay, which the Egyptians placed under the head of their dead. They believed it would magically cause the head and body to be enveloped in flames or radiance, thus making the deceased divine. The hypocephalus itself symbolized the eye of Re or Horus (the sun), and the scenes portrayed on it relate to the Egyptian concept of the resurrection and life after death.

  To the Egyptians, the daily rising and setting of the sun was a vivid symbol of the resurrection. The hypocephalus itself represented all that the sun encircles—the whole world. The upper portion represented the world of men and the day sky; the lower portion (the part with the cow) represents the nether world and the night sky (Rhodes, *The Joseph Smith Hypocephalus*, 1).

- Just as there are numerous documents like Facsimile No. 1, many documents similar to Facsimile No. 2 have been found. These documents are referred to as the Eye of Ra, Horus, or Osiris (Bonwick, *Egyptian Belief and Modern Thought*, 210; Budge, *The Book of the Dead*, 203; Faulkner, *The Ancient Egyptian Coffin Texts*, 1:234). The name Osiris is written with the sign of the Wadjet-Eye. The hypocephalus relates to this eye, which signifies consummate knowledge (Griffiths, *The Origins of Osiris and His Cult*, 88; Nibley, *The Three Facsimiles from the Book of Abraham*, 66). Strictly speaking, the hypocephalus is the pupil of the eye, and it is significant that the hieroglyphic name of Ra is a sun-circle with a pupil-like dot in the center (see Gardiner, *Egyptian Grammar*, 485).

- The linen and plaster hypocephali have figures and inscriptions, generally in black outline on a yellow ground (Birch, *Proceedings of the Society of Biblical Archaeology*, 37). Some hypocephali have been found drawn directly on the mummy wrappings on the top of the head (Lyon, *Appreciating Hypocephali as Words of Art and Faith*, Figure 11: Cha-Kheper, Musee Du Louvre, Inv.: E26834a), while others were drawn on papyrus and rolled up with other sacred writings, such as was the case with Facsimile No. 2 when the Prophet Joseph first viewed it in Kirtland in July 1835 (Smith, *History of the Church*, 2:348–49).

- These documents were placed with the deceased for the purpose of retaining warmth in the body until the resurrection, and are associated with the course of the sun as it points to the immortality of the soul (Birch, *Proceedings of the Society of Biblical Archaeology*, 37, 126–27; "Notes," *Archaeologia*, 174). The Egyptians believed that this disk-shaped object would magically cause the head and body to be enveloped in flames or radiance, thus making the deceased divine (Rhodes, *The Joseph Smith Hypocephalus*, 1). The persons for whom they were made had upon them the name Osiris and were considered his followers, and were hopeful of obtaining an inheritance in the heavenly Heliopolis (sun-city) of Ra or Osiris (Rhodes, *The Joseph Smith Hypocephalus*, 13). These documents were held as sacred and were to be kept secret (Birch, "Notes," *Archaeologia*, 174).

- The hypocephalus actually represents a globe or a sphere. This idea was difficult to demonstrate on a flat surface; therefore, special conventions were used (Nibley, "Facsimile No. 2," Forum).

- Some have criticized Joseph Smith because Egyptologists say the hypocephali came into use between the XXVIth and the XXXth dynasties (343–64 B.C. (Birch, *Proceedings of the Society of Biblical Archaeology*, 37), while Abraham lived about 1800 B.C. (Draper, *The Pearl of Great Price*, 238). Yet, they say, "none are inscribed with any royal name, so as to fix their date precisely, but the names and persons for who they were made, and the coffins of the mummies from which they were taken, seem to point to that period" (Birch, *Proceedings of the Society of Biblical Archaeology*, 37). There is, however, one hypocephalus that has a royal name in it that dates back at least to 940 B.C. That is our Facsimile No. 2, for in it is a prayer that life be granted to the "Osiris Shishaq" (Figure 8), which is the name of one of the Egyptian pharaohs who ruled in the XXII dynasty, the "Sheshonq I" or Shishak of the Bible (2 Chronicles 12:9). While this does not necessarily help us date the document back to Abraham, it shows that all the information is not yet in.

- There is one more thing to consider. We have shown that the hypocephalus was called the Eye of Horus. It should be noted that the Red dsr.t-bee Crown of Lower Egypt (Nibley, *Abraham in Egypt*, 241), which existed from the beginning of Egyptian history, was called the eye of Horus. In the earliest texts of the Egyptians, the Pyramid Texts, it is said, "O King, I provide you with the Eye of Horus, the Red Crown rich in power and many-natured, that it may protect you, O King, just as it protects Horus; may it set your power O King . . . (and) raise you up, O King; that (it) may guide you to your mother Nūt that she may take your hand" (Faulkner, *The Ancient Egyptian Pyramid Texts*, 157–58). From this it is plain to see that this crown played the same role as the hypocephalus: to raise up its wearer and bring him into the heavenly city of Heliopolis. Nut, called the "bosom of the gods" (Bonwick, *Egyptian Belief and Modern Thought*, 115; Budge, *The Gods of the Egyptians*, 1:200–201) and associated with the bee (Faulkner, *The Ancient Egyptian Pyramid Texts*, 142) was the embodiment of that sacred city (Faulkner, *The Ancient Egyptian Pyramid Texts*, 240; Budge, *The Gods of the Egyptians*, 2:106–7), which incidentally is named three times in our facsimile. This reminds us of the words of Paul, that "Jerusalem which is above is free, which is the mother of us all" (Galatians 4:26).

Now to the point. The Red dsr.t (deseret) crown was a flat circular cap, which in the very act of putting it on would be like placing a hypocephalus on the head. Was this sacred crown ever inscribed with hypocephalus-type markings? That remains to be seen. One thing is certain: the principle of the hypocephalus has always existed in the concept of the Red Crown.

(Silverman,
Masterpieces,
126)

What meaning is given to this document by the Prophet Joseph Smith or Abraham?

- Just as with Facsimile No. 1, the explanations given of this document are not those of Abraham but of the Prophet Joseph Smith. He is the one showing us how they relate to Abraham. The only thing he says about the document as a whole is taken from his journal on March 4, 1842: "At my office exhibiting the Book of Abraham in the original to Brother Reuben Hedlock, so that he might take the size of the several plates or cuts, and prepare the blocks for the 'Times and Seasons,' and also gave instruction concerning the arrangement of the writing on the large cut, illustrating the principles of astronomy" (Hunter, *Pearl of Great Price Commentary,* 33).
- Joseph did not give explanations for all the parts of this document. When we look closely, we see that he explained only the figures and none of the writing. As we explained earlier, the figures have their own Egyptian meaning, but they are utilized in this instance to convey the message of Abraham. We have reason to believe that parts of the document were damaged. Joseph made some restorations. (We talk about this later.) When he did so, he was only concerned with a restoration that related to Abraham and not with the message that was originally intended by the Egyptians. In relationship to the writing, he differentiated between lines that could eventually be understood by the world and those that could only be understood in the temple, such as Figure 8.

If we look at this Egyptian document as an imitation, what gospel principles can we see in it?

 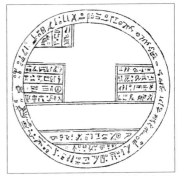

Figures 1, 2, 3, 4, 5, 6, 7, 22, 23: translated by the Prophet

Figures 8, 9, 10, 11, 12, 13, 14, 15, 16, 17, 18, 19, 20, 21: not translated by the Prophet

- Before we think about this document, let's take a minute just to look at it—really look at it. What do you see? Knowing that this document represents the eye of God, what things does it suggest? Here are some possibilities:
- The eye is often associated with the mind. Looking into a person's eye, it is said, is like looking into a person's mind. Looking at the eye in this document suggests that we are seeing things that are in the Lord's mind. Notice that the eye is dilated. What causes an eye to dilate? Most people would say light, but the reverse is true. God is looking at you and me—and every single member of the human family—and compared with him, we are in the darkness. Now, He doesn't have to look at us—He wants to, and His dilated eye shows forth the promises that He has reserved in His mind for each of us. That is why these documents relate to the idea of the resurrection and the immortality of the soul. Significantly, the Lord says, "mine eyes are upon you. I am in your midst and ye cannot see me" (D&C 38:7). He is always looking at us. Perhaps that is one of the messages He wants us to understand by putting His "eye" in the pages of our scriptures.
- The sun is one of the scriptural symbols of God, "whose glory" it says, "the sun of the firmament is written of as being typical" (D&C 76:70). It also says, "he is in the sun, and the light of the sun, and the power thereof by which it was made" (D&C 88:7). Facsimile 2 is associated with the sun and its journey across the sky. Is it any wonder then that these things represent the invitation to "follow the Son, with full purpose of heart"? (2 Nephi 31:13). And those who do so will "shine forth as the sun in the kingdom of their Father" (Matthew 13:43).

(Patrick, *All Colour Book*, 52)

- Facsimile 2 is a circle with a special marking on the god who is shown at the very center (Figure 1).

  It is a like an X (Rawlinson, *History of Ancient Egypt,* 1:332), but it is actually a loop that encircles the neck of the god (Patrick, *All Colour Book of Egyptian Mythology,* 52; Gardiner, *Egyptian Grammar,* 523). It can be seen above on the god Osiris. X marks the spot, but what spot? The scriptures give us a hint. Speaking of God, they say, "All things are round about him; and he is . . . round about all things" (D&C 88:41) A symbol represents that principle—a sphere with a dot in the center, a sphere in which God is not only the circumference but also the center.

  If we were to represent that on a flat surface, it would simply be a circle with a center dot. It was pointed out earlier that this symbol is the hieroglyphic sign for the name Ra, who is the god of Egypt

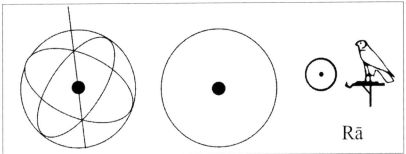

Sphere circle (Budge, *An Egyptian Hieroglyphic Dictionary,* 1:418b)

  who has the sun as his symbol.
- A great circle with a center point suggests the idea of a center planet on which God resides (see Facsimile 2:1) and gives meaning to expressions such as "thou hast taken Zion to thine own bosom, from all thy creations, from all eternity to all eternity" (Moses 7:31); Christ being "in the bosom of the Father, even from the beginning" (D&C 76:13); and God sitting "upon his throne, who is in the bosom of eternity, who is in the midst of all things" (D&C 88:13).

  It is of extreme interest to go through the scriptures and observe the number of times that the Lord, in His teaching methods and doctrine, demonstrates the idea of Himself as teacher in the center and those to be taught either looking to Him, or gathering around Him in a circle (see Abraham 3:21; 3 Nephi 27:14; 3 Nephi 15:9;

JS–Matthew 1:27; Moses 7:62–63; D&C 101:22; D&C 42:36; D&C 42:9; D&C 39:22). Of course, the tribes of Israel around the tabernacle, and the oxen surrounding the baptismal fonts in the Temples, and sacred prayer circles are examples, demonstrative not only of the work of the Savior but also that all things are centered in Him.

- If Facsimile No. 2 represents the traveling of the sun across the sky, we might wonder how it represents the journey that man must take in following the Son. This will become apparent as we go along.

Figure 1

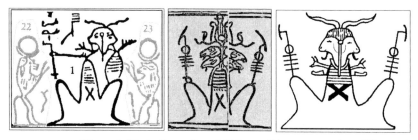

(Figure 1; Birch, *Proceedings,* 6:106; possible reconstruction of Figure 1)

What does this figure represent in the world of the Egyptians?

- 1. A seated deity with two (or four) ram's heads. He is holding in his hand the symbols of life (*ankh*), dominion (*was*), and stability (*djed*). On either side of the god are two apes (numbers 22 and 23) with horned moon-disks on their heads, in an attitude of adoration. There are also two serpents, one on either side of the seated deity (note: figures 22 and 23 are treated separately). The god is sitting at the center of the hypocephalus, which represents the world (Rhodes, *The Joseph Smith Hypocephalus,* 7).
- This seated figure represents god as the creator, either Amon-Re or Khnum. When thus depicted with four heads, this god united within himself the attributes of the gods Re (the sun), Shu (light), Geb (the earth), and Osiris (the next world and the resurrection), and represented the primeval creative force (Rhodes, *The Joseph Smith Hypocephalus,* 7).
- From an ink drawing of Facsimile 2 found among the papers of Joseph Smith, we gather that the original was likely damaged

(Ashment, "The Facsimiles," *Sunstone*, 39)

when Joseph received it.

The damage was largely in the middle, which one would expect if it had been used under the head of a deceased person, as prescribed. However, we do not know if Facsimile 2 was ever used in that way. Others have been found with similar damage (see British Museum Hypocephalus 37909.) Some of the crumbled and missing pieces may have been found between the sheets of papyri—the reconstruction by Joseph Smith seems to show pieces placed in the figure where they wouldn't normally be found. Nevertheless, Joseph, having never seen another picture like it, reconstructed it sufficiently to suit the message of Abraham.

(Saleh, *The Egyptian Antiquties*, 889)

- In most other hypocephali that have been found, this figure has four heads, two bodies, ram's horns, an atef crown with sun-disk, two bodies, and two large scepters. However, other variations also exist, including four heads, ram horns and no crown; two heads, ram's horns and no crown; two heads, no ram's horn, and a crown; four heads and only one side of the double body; a sun-disk crown; and a sun-disk crown with a serpent in it. Most hold scepters, one does not. Some wear a single crown, others wear a triple crown.

What's going on here? Why the discrepancy? It is a single

principle expressed in a variety of ways. Often it was a preference of the scribe, and more often than that, was dictated by available space. One thing seems to be constant: there are at least two heads, and they are the ram looking into both of the dimensions of eternity.

• In Facsimile No. 1 we saw Osiris rising from the dead to take his place in the center of eternity. We pointed out that the four canopic gods represented the four cardinal directions and expressed the idea of a central gathering. As Osiris arises, he is sometimes shown with four bars or rungs across his body. This indicates that he is about to take his place in the center of eternity where the four directions meet.

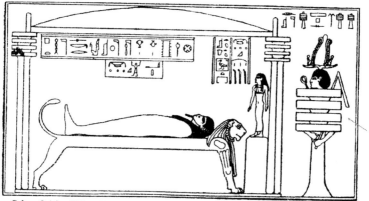

Seker-Osiris of Memphis ; the goddess at the head is Isis.   Osiris-Ṭeṭ in Busiris.
Mariette, *Dendérah*, IV, 71.

(Budge, *Osiris and the Egyptian Resurrection,* 2:35)

When he takes his place, he becomes the great ram-god called Khnum. The ram, of course, is a symbol of virility, power, and resurrection (Watterson, *The Gods of Ancient Egypt,* 73; Bonwick, *Egyptian Belief and Modern Thought,* 103). To bring all these things together, he is given four heads, which not only signify the cardinal directions but also effectively turn our flat facsimile into a sphere, in which he is the center.

• The ram-god Khnum (Amon-Ra or Osiris) was thought to be a potter, who fashioned man on a potter's wheel (Nibley, *The Three Facsimiles from the Book of Abraham,* 43). He is identified variously by different Egyptologists as Ra, Amen, Amun-Ra, Khnum, Khnum-Ra (Num-Ra—representing the spirit of the four elements, the soul of the material world, and the spirit of the four winds or four cardinal points) (Birch, *Proceedings of the Society of Biblical Archaeology*, 128). Other interpretations include "the god of many names," "the god of four faces on one neck," Ra-Horus, and Ptah-Socharis-Osiris (Ptah-Seker-Osiris) (Birch, *Proceedings of the Society of Biblical Archaeology*, 38, 128, 145, 171). When thus depicted, with four heads, this god united within himself the attributes of the gods Re (the sun), Shu (light or air), Geb (the earth), and Osiris (god of the next world and the resurrection), and represented the primeval creative force (Rhodes, *The Joseph Smith Hypocephalus*, 7). He sits in the center with heads joined, looking to the left and to the right, positioned on two back-to-back bodies with knees extended, holding a scepter (Harris, *The Facsimilies in the Book of Abraham*, 60).

"He rises up from the Solar Mount, with four heads lighting up heaven and earth with his rays, and he cometh as the Nile to give life to the universe . . . the giver of Light, issuing from the Solar Mount" (Birch, *Proceedings of the Society of Biblical Archaeology*, 145.) "The word ram in all Semitic languages means high" (Nibley, *Teachings of the Book of Mormon*, 431), and the ram in the highest place is "the most high."

- Among the myriad of names of this great god (Osiris) was the curious, "I am that I am" (Bonwick, *Egyptian Belief and Modern Thought*, 395).
- The scepters he holds, the Waś, Djed, and Ankh, represent respectively dominion, stability, and life (Rhodes, *The Joseph Smith Hypocephalus*, 7).

   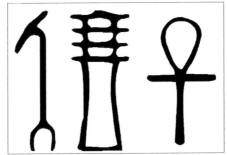

(Birch, *Proceed-
ings*, 6:106)   (Gardiner, *Egyptian Grammar*, 559)

- As mentioned above, Ptah-Seker-Osiris is one of the names of our central facsimile figure. He is said to have come forth from the Great Temple of the Aged One in Annu (Heliopolis) (Budge, *The Book of the Dead,* 482). This god was called the "triune god of the resurrection" for he embodied three gods in one, which were the principles of:

a.) Ptah (Pteh) a representation of the heart and tongue of the gods, the "great god, who came into being in the beginning, he who resteth upon the darkness," "the father of beginnings," "the Word—in the beginning was the Word," who created all things in the beginning (Budge, *An Egyptian Hiero-glyphic Dictionary,* 2:254b; Rawlinson, *History of Ancient Egypt,* 1:336; Aldred, *The Egyptians,* 84).

b.) Seker, the principle of death and the powers of darkness associated with Set, the mortal enemy and murderer of Osiris.

c.) Osiris, the resurrected one and the giver of everlasting life (see Budge, *The Gods of the Egyptians,* 1:502–4, 507–8).

The god Ptah, Lord of the cubit, the symbol of trught and justice (Bonwick, *Egyptian Thought,* 107–10, 212).

Ptah-Seker-Osiris was the Egyptian Logos (Bonwick, *Egyptian Belief and Modern Thought,* 404–5; see page 78 of this book) through whom and by whom the worlds are made. A temple to him was erected by Menes, the first king, thus indicating the high antiquity of his worship. He is the giver of life and the good god. He is the latent germ to be developed in perfect beauty and fitness. He is Lord of the Cubit; he is Osiris purified. He makes all things in perfect manner. Egyptians called the wisdom of the First Intellect, Ptah. Ptah is divine wisdom, scattering the stars in immensity.

In the ritual for the dead there is this prayer: Homage to Ptah, Lord of Justice, divine soul, living in truth, creator of gods and men, immortal Lord, who illumines the worlds. "The solar disk of heaven is his eye, illuminating the two worlds with his rays—Generator of all men, he produces their substance.—Thou art without father, being engendered by thy will, Thou art without mother, being born by the renewal of thine own substance from whom proceeds substance" (Bonwick, *Egyptian Belief and Modern Thought*, 107–10).

- The cubit, represented by the squared arm of Amon below, relates to the ka, the Egyptian sign of the stretched-out or reaching arm. It was associated with the idea of embracing, or "folding in the arms" (Gardiner, *Egyptian Grammar*, 453; Budge, *An Egyptian Hieroglyph-*

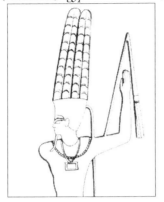

(Keel, *The Symbolism*, 287)   (Quirke, *Ancient Egyptian Religion*, 66)

ic Dictionary, 2:693a), which formed part of the rites of initiation.
- The cubit was also the symbol of Maat, "the embodiment of truth and justice, kingship and social order" (Watterson, *The Gods of Ancient Egypt*, 36).
- The Khnum figure is God at the center of the universe possessing all power, truth, and glory. He is the divine father and the generator of all things. Because this god was such a conglomerate of gods, it is interesting to discover that he is actually a council of gods. "He (Osiris) is the leader of the gods . . . who commands the Great Council (in heaven)" (Nibley, *Abraham in Egypt*, 141–42).

What meaning is given to this figure by the Prophet or Abraham?

- "Kolob, signifying the first creation, nearest to the celestial, or the residence of God. First in government, last pertaining to the measurement of time. The measurement according to celestial time, which celestial time signifies one day to a cubit. One day in Kolob is equal to a thousand years according to the measurement of this earth, which is called by the Egyptians Jah-oh-eh" (Explanation: Figure 1).

- Joseph Smith's statement agrees well with the Egyptian symbolism of god endowed with the primeval creative force seated at the center of the universe. The name Kolob is right at home in this context. The word most likely derives from the common Semitic root QLB, which has the basic meaning of "heart, center, middle" (Arabic qalb "heart, center"; Hebrew "middle, midst," "to draw near"; Egyptian mqAb "in the midst of"). In fact, qalb forms part of the Arabic names of several of the brightest stars in the sky, including Antares, Regulus, and Canopus (Rhodes, *The Joseph Smith Hypocephalus*, 8).

- *Joseph Smith's Egyptian Alphabet and Grammar* speaks of three of the grand governing stars and planets in the universe (Oliblish, Enish-go-on-dosh, and Kai e van rash) and the work it has taken the prophets to discover them, even though they had use of the Urim and Thummim. Joseph said these "are the three grand central powers that govern all the other creations, which have been sought out by the most aged of all the fathers, since the beginning of the creation, by means of the Urim and Thummim." He also spoke of Kolob, which "signifies the first great grand governing fixed star which is the fartherest that ever has been discovered by the fathers which was discovered by Methusela and also by Abraham," and that it signifies "the wonder of Abraham the eldest of all the Stars, the greatest body of the heavenly bodies that ever was discovered by man" (Smith, *Joseph Smith's Egyptian Alphabet and Grammar*, 24, 32, 34).

- The vision of Abraham contains an object lesson for Abraham—and for us. The Lord showed Abraham the stars and planets and how they were organized, and then He showed Abraham the intelligences that He had organized. The intelligences, the record discloses, are organized in the same way as the planets. They are hierarchical, receiving light from those above and giving light to those below. In the scale of planets, one was greater than all the rest, and so it is with the intelligences. The great planet is Kolob and the great intelligence is Christ. Following is a chart showing the scriptural relationship between the two as the object lesson discloses.

The Vision of Abraham (Abraham 3)

If we look at this Egyptian figure as an imitation, what gospel principles can we see in it?

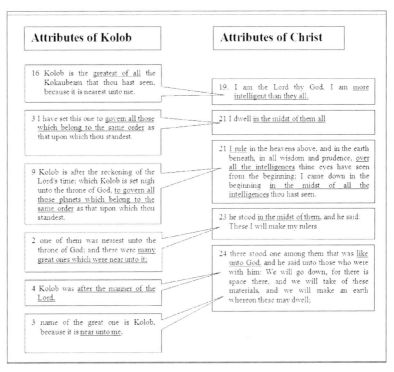

Attributes of Kolob	Attributes of Christ
16 Kolob is the greatest of all the Kokaubeam that thou hast seen, because it is nearest unto me.	19. I am the Lord thy God, I am more intelligent than they all.
3 I have set this one to govern all those which belong to the same order as that upon which thou standest.	21 I dwell in the midst of them all
9 Kolob is after the reckoning of the Lord's time; which Kolob is set nigh unto the throne of God, to govern all those planets which belong to the same order as that upon which thou standest.	21 I rule in the heavens above, and in the earth beneath, in all wisdom and prudence, over all the intelligences thine eyes have seen from the beginning; I came down in the beginning in the midst of all the intelligences thou hast seen.
2 one of them was nearest unto the throne of God; and there were many great ones which were near unto it;	23 he stood in the midst of them, and he said: These I will make my rulers
4 Kolob was after the manner of the Lord,	24 there stood one among them that was like unto God, and he said unto those who were with him: We will go down, for there is space there, and we will take of these materials, and we will make an earth whereon these may dwell;
3 name of the great one is Kolob, because it is near unto me.	

• It is not an accident that the character chosen to represent God in the center of the universe is a ram, which signifies resurrection. We read that all "shall be brought forth by the resurrection of the dead, through the triumph and the glory of the Lamb, who was slain, who was in the bosom of the Father before the worlds were made" (D&C 76:39). Lest we should be put off by the more crude ram rather than lamb, let us not forget the hymn that we sing so often, "Once a meek and lowly Lamb, Now the Lord, the great I Am" (*Hymns,* no. 196).

Speaking of I Am, the Savior says of himself, "Listen to the voice of him who is from all eternity to all eternity, the Great I Am, even Jesus Christ" (D&C 39:1). We saw earlier that this was also one of the names of Osiris. To further emphasize the centrality of God, the Prophet Joseph Smith said, "The past, the present, and the future were and are, with Him, one eternal 'now'" (Smith, *Teachings,* 220). In addition to this, the Lord's superior intelligence was made known to Abraham in his great vision when the Lord said, "These two facts do exist, that there are two spirits, one being more intelligent than the other; there shall be another more intelligent than they; I am the Lord thy God, I am more intelligent than they all. . . .I dwell in the midst of them all; I now, therefore, have come down unto thee to declare unto thee the works which my hands have made, wherein my wisdom excelleth them all, for I rule in the heavens above, and in the earth beneath, in all wisdom and prudence, over all the intelligences thine eyes have seen from the beginning; I came down in the beginning in the midst of all the intelligences thou hast seen" (Abraham 3:19, 21).

- Like Khnum, the Lord is declared to be a potter by Isaiah who said, "But now, O Lord, thou art our father; we are the clay, and thou our potter; and we all are the work of thy hand" (Isaiah 64:8; see also Revelation 2:27; Jeremiah 18:6).
- Like Khnum, God is "the Most High God." Melchizedek in blessing Abraham said, "Blessed be the most high God, which hath delivered thine enemies into thy hand" (Genesis 14:20; 1 Nephi 11:6).
- Like Osiris, God holds a scepter. He said, "there was joy in heaven when my servant Warren bowed to my scepter, and separated himself from the crafts of men" (D&C 106:6).
- Like Ptah-Seker-Osiris, the Savior is literally the triune god of the resurrection (three in one), for His mission had three parts. His pre-earth life, as the Word or Logos of God, the Creator, the opener and beginner (see John 1:1–3, 14); His mortal and dying mission; and His resurrection.
- Like Ptah-Seker-Osiris coming forth from the heavenly city of Heliopolis, the Savior has come down to us from that great city of the Heavenly Jerusalem, which is in the "bosom" of eternity, and he desires for us to inherit it with him (see D&C 38:4; Moses 7:31, 47, 69).
- Like Ptah-Seker-Osiris, the Savior is the illuminator of worlds (see D&C 88:7–13). He is in the sun and the light of the sun; he is in the moon and the light of the moon; he is in the stars and the light of them.
- Ptah-Seker-Osiris is portrayed as being "without father" and "without mother." This is surely an attempt to link the god with priesthood, for it is actually the Priesthood after the Order of the Son of God, that is "without father, without mother" (Hebrews 7:3), and "without beginning of days or end of years, being prepared from eternity to all eternity" (Alma 13:7).

- The cubit is a unique unit of measure. It is based on arm length and is the distance from the tip of the elbow to the tip of the middle finger. It is roughly eighteen inches. The symbol of the cubit is represented every time we put our right arm to the square to sustain our leaders or to enter into sacred covenants (see D&C 88:119–20). It is a measurement upon which many holy things are constructed. We see it in Genesis 6 (the ark of Noah), Exodus 25 (the Ark of the Covenant of Moses), Exodus 27 (the Tabernacle of Moses), 1 Kings 6 (the Temple of Solomon) Ezekiel 41 (the temple in the vision of Ezekiel), and Revelation 21 (the city of New Jerusalem). Because it represents the arm, it suggests the idea of reaching, of embracing, of covenanting, and gathering of all things eventually into the bosom of God. It is a visible sign and token of the covenants of gathering that God has made to Israel. Various scriptures speak of the arm of the Lord being stretched out or that it is not shortened (see 2 Nephi 28:32; D&C 35:8).

We learn in the explanation to Figure 1 of Facsimile 2 that one day with the Lord, which is a thousand years of our time, is to Him equal to one cubit. This equates time and distance. In some manner, a thousand years of time is equal to eighteen inches of distance. Could that mean that when we lived with the Lord in heaven, we lived in an environment so advanced that in the time it took for us to move the distance of one cubit (about the space it takes to turn halfway around) a thousand years according to mortal time would have passed? This would mean that in coming to earth, we are on an accelerated, fast-forward merry-go-round, and that the whole thing passes with God in the twinkling of an eye. And when we return to heaven, it will appear as if we had hardly been gone at all.

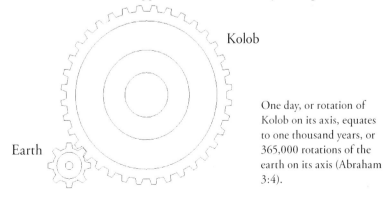

Kolob

Earth

One day, or rotation of Kolob on its axis, equates to one thousand years, or 365,000 rotations of the earth on its axis (Abraham 3:4).

Figure 2

(Figure 2; Lyon, *Appreciating Hypocephali,* 13; drawing of Figure 2)

What does this figure represent in the world of the Egyptians?

- A two-headed deity wearing the double-plumed crown of Amon with ram's horns mounted on it. On his shoulders are jackal heads, and he is holding the jackal standard. To his right is an altar with offerings on and around it. In most hypocephali, he is holding the ankh, or symbol of life, in his right hand (Rhodes, *The Joseph Smith Hypocephalus,* 8).

- This is Amon-Re, the chief god of the Egyptian pantheon; the two heads illustrate the hidden and mysterious power of Amon (his name in Egyptian means the Hidden One) combined with the visible and luminous power of Re. This is clearly the god mentioned in chapter 162 of the Book of the Dead (the chapter describing the construction and use of the hypocephalus), who wears the double-plumed crown. The jackals on his shoulders, as well as the jackal standard he holds, are symbols of the god Wepwawet, the Opener of the Way, meaning of the year, of the king in his conquests, of the dead through the dangers of hereafter to the throne of Osiris, where they would be judged (Rhodes, *The Joseph Smith Hypocephalus,* 8).

- We have seen that Figure 1 represents god in the center of the universe. This figure now represents him on the move. In this second part of a heavenly drama, He becomes Logos, the Firstborn of heaven, the "Divine Word, by whom all things were made, and who though from God, was God," "the first person after himself (god) uncreated, infinite, ruling over all things that were made by him," "the Second One . . . produced from the First One . . . called forth for the avowed purpose of creating and governing all things; associating to 'Messiah,'" "the love which the Divine Principle conceives for the first product of its will," and "the eternal generation of the Son of God . . . the Eternal Sonship" (Bonwick, *Egyptian Belief and Modern Thought,* 157, 402, 404–5, 424). It is Amon, the supreme god of Thebes, identified with Ra, the Sun, under the name of Amon-Ra.

The two heads represent the rising and setting sun. He is the Hidden One, "the personification of the hidden and unknown creative power . . . associated with the . . . primeval . . . god in the creation of the world and all that is in it." The name Amon means "what is hidden" or that which is not seen and not known. He was a combination of "the unseen mysterious principle of Amon and the visible and brilliant power of Ra" (Harris, *The Facsimilies of the Book of Abraham,* 63).

- On the Ashmolean figure (pg. 78), the feathers of Maat (truth) can clearly be seen under the jackal heads on the shoulders. The god says, "You shall see me in my great Atef-crowns . . . my image of Truth on my shoulder" (Faulkner, *The Ancient Egyptian Coffin Texts,* 1:233). He holds the Ankh symbol in his right hand.

ankh symbol

- The vertical line of hieroglyphs on the right side of Figure 2 (below), read, "The name of this Mighty God" (Rhodes, *The Joseph Smith Hypocephalus,* 3, 5).

(Rhodes, *The Joseph Smith Hypocephalus,* 3, 5)

What meaning is given to this figure by the Prophet Joseph Smith or Abraham?

- "Stands next to Kolob, called by the Egyptians Oliblish, which is the next grand governing creation near to the celestial or the place where God resides; holding the key of power also, pertaining to other planets; as revealed from God to Abraham, as he offered sacrifice upon an altar, which he had built unto the Lord" (Explanation: Figure 2).
- From Figure 4, the Prophet adds, "The measuring of the time of Oliblish . . . is equal with Kolob in its revolution and in its measuring of time" (Explanation: Figure 4).
- The offering table covered with lotus flowers in the corner of figure 2 is unique and does not appear in other hypocephali. The ink

drawing from the *Joseph Smith's Egyptian Alphabet and Grammar*, referred to earlier, is damaged where this table appears. No information exists to explain how the restoration of the figure came about.

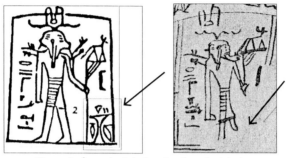

Figure 2, from the ink drawing found with the
alphabet and grammar.

If we look at this Egyptian figure as an imitation, what gospel principles can we see in it?

From the explanations of the Prophet Joseph, it would seem that the offering table with its lotus flowers is intended to represent the sacrifice on the altar by Abraham, which precipitated the revelations contained in this document. What sacrifice would Abraham have offered? Would it not have been a lamb in the likeness of the sacrifice of Jesus Christ? Christ was "the Lamb, who was slain, who was in the bosom of the Father before the worlds were made" (D&C 76:39) and Enoch exclaimed that "the Lamb is slain from the foundation of the world" (Moses 7:47). In other words, the plan of the Father commenced in the person of the Son, who had not only obtained the power of the Father but also proceeded forth as the atoning one, as if he had already been slain. If we liken His mission from that moment on to Figure 2, we can see the following things.

- Like the two-headed Amon-Ra and the two-feathered crown, the Savior had the power to comprehend past and future. He is the one "who was, and is from all eternity to all eternity" (Mosiah 3:5).
- Like the ram's horns, he is the "Most High God" (3 Nephi 4:32).
- Like the holder of the jackal standard, he is the "opener of the way," and like the jackal heads on his shoulders and the Ankh symbol in his hand, he holds the keys to open and shut. "I will commit thy *government into his hand* . . . And the *key* of the house of David will I *lay upon his shoulder;* so he shall *open,* and none shall *shut;* and he shall *shut,* and none shall *open*" (Isaiah 22:21–22; emphasis

added). The Prophet Joseph terms this "holding the key of power" (Explanation: Figure 2).

- Like Amon-Ra, he is the Hidden One. "Never have I showed myself unto man whom I have created" (Ether 3:15). "No man knoweth that the Son is the Father, and the Father is the Son, but him to whom the Son will reveal it" (JST Luke 10:23).

- As Amon-Ra, he is the Divine Word of the Father, the Logos, who goes forth in first person as if he is the Father, "the Son of God, the Father of heaven and earth, the Creator of all things from the beginning" (Mosiah 3:8) "And his name is called The Word of God" (Revelation 19:13).

- The feathers on the crown and the feathers on the shoulder symbolize Maat, the truth, which is really two truths, the truth past and the truth future. "Truth is knowledge of things as they are, and as they were, and as they are to come" (D&C 93:24). "I am . . . the Lord, which is, and which was, and which is to come" (Revelation 1:8). "I am the way, the truth, and the life" (John 14:6). "He received a fulness of truth, yea, even of all truth" (D&C 93:26).

- Like the offering table and the lotus flower, the Savior has offered His all on the altar and through that offering, new life has burst forth like the seeds from the pod of the lotus plant to take root in new soil, "a tree springing up unto everlasting life" (Alma 32:41).

(Budge, *From Fetish to God*, 100)

- The name Amon-Ra is instructive because it lends itself to a likeness of the name of God in the pure language of Adam. Elder Orson Pratt said, "There is one revelation that . . . is given in questions and answers. The first question is, 'What is the name of God in the pure language?' The answer says 'Ahman.' 'What is the name of the Son of God?' Answer, 'Son Ahman" (in *Journal of Discourses,* 2:342–43). The Savior calls himself Son Ahman twice (see D&C 78:20; D&C 95:17). Since the Egyptians imitated the things of Adam, we suppose that they also used the name of God from his language, which they wrote as Amen (Budge, *An Egyptian Hieroglyphic Dictionary,* 1:51b). (Because the Egyptians wrote no vowels, it is spelled Amen, Amon, or Amun by Egyptologists.)

The Egyptians used a compound name in relation to Amon. They called the part of god that is hidden, Amon and that part of him that is manifest, or visible, Ra, or the Sun (Rhodes, *The Joseph Smith Hypocephalus,* 8), hence the compound name Amon-Ra. This name surely is an imitation of Ahman-Son or Son-Ahman. The substitution of Sun for Son is a natural one, and we see it in the scriptures, for instance, Sun of Righteousness (see Malachi 4:2) and Son of Righteousness (see 2 Nephi 26:9). If these things are true, our Figure 2 becomes a most enlightening treatise on the majesty and mission of Ahman revealing Himself through His Son as Son Ahman.

Figure 3

What does this figure represent in the world of the Egyptians?

- This figure is a hawk-headed Ra with the sun disk on his head, seated on the solar bark. On either side of him is a Wedjat-eye. In his hand, he holds the Was-scepter, symbol of dominion, and in front of him is an altar with a lotus blossom on it. Ra seated in his bark represents the sun in its daily journey across the sky and symbolizes resurrection and rebirth, since the sun was thought to die and be reborn each day. The lotus on the altar in front of him is also symbolic of rebirth and the rising sun. The Wedjet-eye was symbolic of light and protection (among other things) (Rhodes, *The Joseph Smith Hypocephalus*, 9).
- An ancient Egyptian writing says, "I have come into thee. My heart watcheth, my head is equipped with the White Crown. I act as the guide of the celestial beings. I make to flourish terrestrial beings. There is joy of heart for the Bull, and for the celestial beings, and for the Company of the Gods. I am the god, the Bull, the Lord of the gods, who maketh his way over the turquoise. O wheat and barley of the nome of the god, I have come into thee. I have come forward. I have lifted [you] up, following the best offerings of the Company of the Gods. I have moored my boat to the tying-up post in the lakes of the celestial beings" (Budge, *The Book of the Dead*, 643).
- "They prepare a path for me, even I who moor with those who are in the Sky and earth. I will sit down, turn around, take my seat, and appear in my flaming glory; I will acclaim my scepter and will flourish by means of my rod (Wand). I have tied my ornament to my neck, the Red Crown is my strength. . . . I have seen my father face to face" (Faulkner, *The Ancient Egyptian Coffin Texts*, 2:230).
- Said to the dead, "Welcome to the fanes (temple)! You are clad in the pure garment of Ptah, in the robe of Hathor. Spacious is your seat in the Bark; you sit in the Ship of God. Fair is your rising like the rising of Ra, you shine like Hathor" (Faulkner, *The Ancient Egyptian Coffin Texts*, 1:56).
- An address by the deified king says, "I row in my seat in the divine ship. I have gone down upon my throne in the divine ship. I control; none being near my throne in the divine ship; I am in control, not being without a boat, my throne being in

the divine ship at Heliopolis" (Nibley, *The Message of the Joseph Smith Papyri*, 138).

Divine Ship

(Rhodes, *The Joseph Smith Hypocephalus*, 3, 5)

What meaning is given to this figure by the Prophet Joseph Smith or Abraham?

- "Is made to represent God, sitting upon his throne, clothed with power and authority; with a crown of eternal light upon his head; representing also the grand Key-words of the Holy Priesthood, as revealed to Adam in the Garden of Eden, as also to Seth, Noah, Melchizedek, Abraham, and all to whom the Priesthood was revealed" (Explanation: Figure 3).

If we look at this Egyptian figure as an imitation, what gospel principles can we see in it?

- The idea of God sailing in a ship brings to mind the scriptures which say, "Sing unto God, sing praises to his name: extol him that *rideth upon the heavens* by his name JAH, and rejoice before him" (Psalm 68:4; emphasis added), or "To him that *rideth upon the heavens of heavens,* which were of old; lo, he doth send out his voice, and that a mighty voice" (Psalm 68:33; emphasis added). Arriving at the throne of God is also viewed as a ship journey: "And *land* their souls, yea, their immortal souls, at the right hand of God in the kingdom of heaven, to sit down with Abraham, and Isaac, and with Jacob, and with all our holy fathers, to go no more out" (Helaman 3:30; emphasis added). The implication is that God, Abraham (who is a god), and the traveler (who is becoming a god) will all sit together in the throne-boat.

- The divine boat of Ra, which makes its journey across the sky, has the shape of a sickle on each end (Gardiner, *Egyptian Grammar,* 516, 499). This shape is symbolic of the goddess Maat, indicating the idea of truth, seeing, and seer as a divine title (Gardiner, *Egyptian Grammar,* 516; Budge, *An Egyptian Hieroglyphic Dictionary,* 1:267a).

(Budge, *An Egyptian Hieroglyphic Dictionary,* 1:266b)

Ma'at, "truth," (Gardiner, *Egyptian Grammar,* 516)

Maa, "seer" (Budge, *An Egyptian Hieroglyphic Dictionary,* 267a)

The word Seer or Maa, above, is written with signs that appear to be two stones or two pupils of an eye. It is also written with the symbol of two regular eyes (Budge, *An Egyptian Hieroglyphic Dictionary,* 1:266a). These eyes of truth are seen on either side of the god in Figure 3. They represent the power of God to comprehend all things past and future, which things are joined together in one represented by the disk crown on his head.

- The word Maat is written most often with the sign of an ostrich feather [below center] (Budge, *The Gods of the Egyptians,* 1:416).

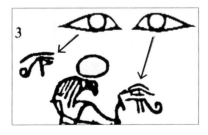

The depiction to the right shows Maat, the truth, as a seer at the prow of the celestial bark of Ra, with the feather of truth on her head, holding the Ankh sign of life and pointing the way (Fix, *Star Maps,* 135). She is equivalent to the two eyes.

(Fix, *Star Maps,* 135)

- The idea of a ship in which God sits, with a crown of eternal light, represented by the disk of the sun, puts us in mind of other ships of light, including the vessels of the Brother of Jared, which had stones of light in them. The record of Ether says that these vessels were built like the ark of Noah (see Ether 6:7). When Noah built the ark, he was told "a window shalt thou make to the ark" (Genesis 6:16). If we look at the footnote to that verse in the LDS scriptures, it says, "Some rabbis believed [that the window] was a precious stone that shone in the ark." Here we have an idea of ships of light sailing forth with precious cargo of men, women, and children, and seed and animals of every kind; "treasure ships" going to a new land. The Jaredites took with them bees, which they called Deseret, for that was the only means of pollinating the seeds that they were taking with them.

The Egyptians in the same likeness also migrated under the sign of the bee. The pharaohs wore the "great crown of Lower Egypt which belongs to Osiris" (Faulkner, *The Ancient Egyptian Coffin Texts*, 1:93). This crown had the antennae of a bee and was called in Egyptian dsrt (Deseret). This teaches that the gods are planters, going forth to plant new worlds. Joseph Smith said, "The design of the ark was given by God, 'a pattern of heavenly things'" (Smith, *Teachings*, 251).

What heavenly things? Early Christian documents speak of God sending forth a ship of light "laden with the riches of the Living" and of Adam's ship from "the treasure of Life" and of Christ coming "like a ship laden with all manner of precious things" (Nibley, *Old Testament and Related Studies*, 188). No wonder Nephi says, "I . . . did not . . . build the ship after the manner of men," (1 Nephi 18:2) for it, too, was a treasure ship with precious cargo going forth to the promised land.

(Budge, *From Fetish to God*, 102)

(Gardiner, *Egyptian Grammar*, 485)

- In the drawing above is a representation of the god Atum, the Ancient of Days, or Adam (Nibley, *Abraham in Egypt*, 215), seated in his boat, which rests upon a symbol of the vault of heaven (above right), indicating that this is a celestial boat. He is in the disk, and in front of him is the sign for follower, as he is in the "following of Osiris" (Gardiner, *Egyptian Grammar*, 513; Budge, *An Egyptian Hieroglyphic Dictionary*, 2:742a). In front of the boat is the lotus, with lotus flowers on the tips of the boat, and the "eye of Horus" on the front, representing, as we have seen, the office of seer, being "the key to the measurement of all things and hence to all knowledge" (Nibley, *The Three Facsimilies from the Book of Abraham*, 65).

- Speaking of ships, President Brigham Young said, "God is at the helm. This is the mighty ship Zion" (Preston Nibley, *Brigham Young*, 293). Of the Zion of Enoch, President Heber C. Kimball said, "God took them and their city . . . and they sailed away like one ship at sea separating from another" (in *Journal of Discourses*, 2:105). The word Zion itself relates to the idea of a ship. In Hebrew it is Tsîyôwn. The first half of the word Tsîy means ship, and the second half ôwn means On, a city of Egypt, or Heliopolis (Hebrew and Chaldee Dictionary, 99, words 6726, 6716; Budge, *The Gods of the Egyptians*, 204). Heliopolis is helio, sun or light, and polis, city, which together mean city of the sun or city of light. With these meanings, the word Zion resolves to "the ship of the city of light." What could be more descriptive of a great city that "sailed" into heaven, and that will "sail" back through space to take its place again where it was taken up?

Descriptions that accompany the word Zion include "to glitter from afar," "a bright object at a distance traveling towards," and being in "splendor, brilliant continually, to the most distant point of view" (Strong, *Strong's Exhaustive Concordance of the Bible*, 80, 5329–32). The idea of a ship speaks of journeys, visits, transporting of sacred cargo, and transplanting between the worlds.

Figure 4

(Harvey, *The Usborne Internet-linked Encylcopedia*, 69)

What does this figure represent in the world of the Egyptians?

- A hawk in mummy wrappings with outspread wings, seated upon a boat. This is Horus-Sokar (Seker), a god, which is symbolized by a mummiform hawk (Rhodes, *The Joseph Smith Hypocephalus*, 9–10). The kingdom of Seker is the "kingdom of death" (Budge, *An Egyptian Hieroglyphic Dictionary*, 1:55a; 2:626b). One outstanding feature of this figure is its outspread wings, which are not normally found in representations of this god. The wings show the personification of the sky as well as emphasizing the emerging of the hawk from his mummy bindings in the resurrection (Rhodes, *The Joseph Smith Hypocephalus*, 9–10).

- Seker in his ship relates to the founding and building of the Egyptian temple and the establishing of its rites, always done by beings who sail from other worlds, and, when their work is done, seem to have sailed away again. Some such space travel is indicated in the Coffin Texts: "He takes the ship of 1000 cubits from end to end, and he sails in it to the stairway of fire." The sky-vessel is called "the ship of 1000 cubits long" (Nibley, *The Message of the Joseph Smith Papyri*, 138; Budge, *The Book of the Dead*, 637). This is the ship of Seker. "Horus (Seker) maketh himself strong like unto a hawk which is one thousand cubits in length, and two thousand cubits in life. He hath equipments with him, he journeyeth on, he cometh to the place where his heart would be, among the Lakes which are in its towns" (Budge, *The Book of the Dead*, 637). This is the journeying of Seker in his hawk-boat (Budge, *An Egyptian Hieroglyphic Dictionary*, 1:211b).

Figure 5

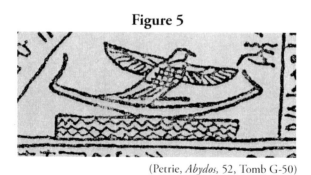

(Petrie, *Abydos*, 52, Tomb G-50)

What meaning is given to this figure by the Prophet or Abraham?

• "Answers to the Hebrew word Raukeeyang, signifying expanse, or the firmament of the heavens; also a numerical figure, in Egyptian signifying one thousand; answering to the measuring of the time of Oliblish, which is equal with Kolob in its revolution and in its measuring of time" (Explanation: Figure 2).

If we look at this Egyptian figure as an imitation, what gospel principles can we see in it?

• On the one hand, this figure represents Satanic evil and death. It is the realm relatively unknown to mortal man and left to the management of God, "who controllest and subjectest the devil, and the dark and benighted dominion of Sheol" (D&C 121:4; Sheol is "the Hebrew name for the abode of departed spirits," i.e., hell; see LDS Bible Dictionary, 773) and the "regions of darkness" (see D&C 77:8; 123:13). It is death in all its deep and horrifying misery, but in this setting, it has none of that gloom and doom, for it depicts the moment of resurrection when all things are released from death's grasp. The figure now speaks a new and exalted language. The representation of the Hawk, speaks light, the boat speaks traversing, the sign for great waters speaks space, and the expansive wings, enlargement and increase. They represent, in effect, "light [which] proceedeth forth from the presence of God to fill the immensity of space" (D&C 88:12) and "the love of God, which sheddeth itself abroad in the hearts of the children of men; wherefore, it is the most desirable above all things" (1 Nephi 11:22). In the principle of lighting, expanding, filling, and enlarging, we observe that the Lord suffered death, "that the resurrection might pass upon all men" (2 Nephi 9:22). In this verse alone is the whole concept of Seker.

What does this figure represent in the world of the Egyptians?

• A cow wearing a sun disk and double plumes with a menat-necklace, the symbol of Hathor. This is the cow mentioned in chapter 162 of the Book of the Dead, which should be drawn on a piece of new papyrus to make a hypocephalus. Hence this picture of a cow is common to almost all hypocephali. "Hathor . . . is a personification of the original waters from which, the whole of creation arose and the one who gave birth to the sun. She . . . also . . . symbolized the sky and is the celestial mother by whom

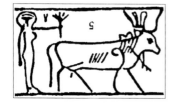

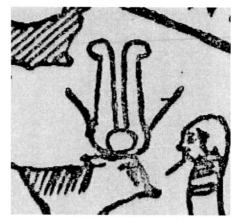

(Lyon, *Appreciating Hypocephali,* 13)

(Birch, *Proceedings,* 6:214)

the sun is reborn each day. (Her) name . . . means, 'Great fullness,' i.e., the primeval waters from which Re, the Sun, first arose. Standing behind the cow is the goddess Wedjat who is holding a lotus blossom, the symbol of rebirth, here indicating the daily and annual renewal of the sun" (Rhodes, *The Joseph Smith Hypocephalus,* 10). The name Hathor means *ht* house, of *hr* Horus (Gardiner, *Egyptian Grammar,* 467, 494), and since Horus was thought to be the "substance of the sun" (Bonwick, *Egyptian Belief and Modern Thought,* 281), she was called the "Mother of Horus," or in other words, the mother of the substance of the sun (Budge, *The Gods of the Egyptians,* 1:429) or the cosmic house of Horus (Nibley, "One Eternal Round," Lecture 11).

• The menat necklace and its counterpoise, which rests on the spine of Hathor, play a considerable part in temple and funerary ritual, where they are related to notions of birth, rebirth, or the passage to a new state. These objects endow the deceased with "the persistence of life, durability, ever-renewed youth." Hathor as the nourishing principle is figured in the form of a cow suckling the royal prince. Every newborn child destined for the throne is assimilated to Horus, the son of Hathor. The menat in the ritual of daily worship is always related to the initial coagulation, or the consolidation of matter, earth, dry land, and so forth, as well as the effect of the first alternation of dilation and contraction at the origins of the world

Ht-hr

(Lamy, *Egyptian Mysteries,* 82, 83, 85).

What meaning is given to this figure by the Prophet Joseph Smith or Abraham?

- "Is called in Egyptian Enish-go-on-dosh; this is one of the govern-ing planets also, and is said by the Egyptians to be the Sun, and to borrow its light from Kolob through the medium of Kae-e-vanrash, which is the grand Key, or, in other words, the governing power, which governs fifteen other fixed planets or stars, as also Floeese or the Moon, the Earth, and the Sun in their annual revolutions. This planet receives its power through the medium of Kli-flos-is-es, or Hah-ko-kau-beam, the stars represented by numbers 22 and 23, receiving light from the revolutions of Kolob" (Explanation: Figure 5).

If we look at this Egyptian figure as an imitation, what gospel prin-ciples can we see in it?

- We see here the Hathor-cow with high horns carrying the sun-disk, showing that she is the bearer of the light. That light, as we have seen, is both global and local, for while she is the substance of the sun itself, she also suckles the newborn king.

  Her functions may be likened to "the light which shineth, which giveth you light (the sun) . . . which is the same light that quickeneth your understand-ings" (D&C 88:11). She is the heav-enly cow, feeding in heavenly pastures of light. When she comes to earth, she

  (Patrick, *All Colour,* 31)

  carries that light in the disk between her horns to give to the youth-ful king, transmitting it to him through her milk, "As newborn babes, desire the sincere milk of the word, that ye may grow there-by" (1 Peter 2:2). It is only through this divine mother-milk that the young prince becomes a true king (Bleeker, *Hathor and Thoth,* 52).
- The Prophet teaches that there are planets above the sun from which the sun gets its light. This is exactly what is portrayed by the Lady with the Wadjet eye, or "the symbol of begotten and

ever-renewing life, expressed in the phenomena of the solar globe." She stands with her head as the sun, filled with the eye of Horus, holding a stylized lotus with three petals over the loins of Hathor. She is giving life and power to the sun. She is making the cow fertile (Nibley, "One Eternal Round," Lecture 11).

• Thinking about an external source giving power to the sun, one writer has said, "The sun is definitely generating light by means of nuclear reactions, but . . . that is not the only source of the sun's light. Accretion (increase by external addition) . . . is actually occurring on the sun. Previously obscure characteristics of the corona of the sun are due to actual material, primarily hydrogen, falling under the influence of gravity into the sun in a spherical distribution with an origin at great, effectively at infinite, distances from the sun. Based on this concept, it can be shown that accretion may actually account for practically all the light of the sun." This may explain how the

(Lyon, *Appreciating Hypocephali*, 13)

sun actually borrows some of its light from external (celestial) sources. Spectroscopic evidence indicates that the temperature increases with distance from the sun from about 11,000° Fahrenheit at the surface to tens of millions of degrees at distances of only one or two solar diameters from the sun. If the sun's interior were the primary source of energy, how does it happen that heat flows from the colder surface of the sun uphill to the tremendously hotter regions (above). This seems contrary to anything natural—heat always flows from the hot to the cold body, not from the cold to the hot one. This, however, is convincing if one considers a model in which the primary energy source is exterior to the sun (Cook, *Science and Mormonism,* 24, 29, 57–58).

• When we think of the principle of dilation and contraction expressed by the menat of Hathor, we can't help but think of the actions of the eye as it dilates and contracts. The dilation expresses the idea of expanding the light and blessings of heaven to the initiate, and the contraction when withholding blessing from those who do not qualify. The Lord sheds forth His spirit upon the world in one instance and withdraws it in another. On the one hand, "light proceedeth forth from the presence of God to fill the immensity of space" (D&C 88:12), and on the other, "I will draw all men unto me, that they may be judged according to their works" (3 Nephi 27:15) and "I will gather together in one all things, both which are in heaven, and which are on earth" (D&C 27:13).

Dilation is also associated with the lady of the Wadjet-eye above. Her head is a sun-disk, but it is filled completely with the dilated eye. She is the bringer of a fulness of power and glory from above. The god Ra says, "I am he who opens his eyes and causes light to be, and if he closes his eyes makes darkness" (Nibley, "One Eternal Round," Lecture 11). Included in this area is also the idea of binding and loosing, opening and closing, rising and setting, ascending and descending, and all things that show a rhythm from less to greater or from greater to less.

Figure 6

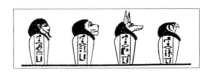

(Rawlinson, *History of Ancient Egypt*, 1:397)

What does this figure represent in the world of the Egyptians?

- These four, standing, mummy-like figures are the four Sons of Horus. They were the gods of the four quarters of the earth and later came to be regarded as presiding over the four cardinal points. They also were guardians of the viscera of the dead, and their images were carved on the four canopic jars into which the internal organs of the dead were placed (Rhodes, *The Joseph Smith Hypocephalus*, 11).
- These are the same as Figures 5–8 in Facsimile No. 1. They are often shown standing on an open lotus flower before the throne of Osiris. The flower stem proceeds forth from the sign of water beneath the throne. Here they signify the earth and all of its functions springing forth from the living waters of Osiris. They also represent his governing power over the earth and all things on the face thereof (Nibley, "A New Look and the Pearl of Great Price,"

Improvement Era, September 1969, 92).

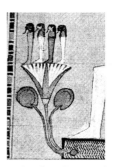

- These four gods held the pillars of heaven and earth in position, and represented the earth in its four cardinal points or quarters, as well as the 'four pure lands' (Harris, *The Facsimilies of the Book of Abraham,* 37).

- The three figures behind the four standing gods are curious indeed. They represent from top to bottom, a leaf, a lion, and a ram or lamb. They appear in other hypocephali, though sometimes in different order.

(Budge, *Osiris and the Egyptian Resurrection,* 1:20)

The graphic and symbolic representation below is one of life moving from the highest to the lowest realms (Nibley, *Figure 6 of Facsimile 2,* 21–22). The leaf or plant gets eaten by the herbivore, and the herbivore gets eaten by the carnivore, then the carnivore gets eaten by the plant. That's Samson's riddle (Judges 14). Out of the killer came strength. The lion dies and rots, and out of him grows the grass and the plants and so forth. This is the life cycle (ibid.). All things here are moving in one direction—down. It is death to which all these things are headed. This is the lowest point on the hypocephalus. Power and life has come down from the center of all things (Figure 1), through each of the figures until this point. All things end here. It is the point where some intervention is needed or all is lost.

Leaf

Lion

Lamb

(Lyon, *Appreciating Hypocephali,* Figure 13)

What meaning is given to this figure by the Prophet Joseph Smith or Abraham?

- "Represents this earth in its four quarters" (Explanation: Figure 6).

If we look at this Egyptian figure as an imitation, what gospel principles can we see in it?

- There is a connection between the four cardinal points represented by the canopic gods and the hieroglyphic sign for city in Egyptian. This symbol and its meaning will be discussed when we study the rim inscriptions.

(Gardiner, *Egyptian Grammar*, 498)

- In this world of quick fixes and fast food, we often forget that we are all headed for death. It is the inevitable reality. It is a dog-eat-dog world, but eventually all will die and become dormant and silent. This moment is captured by Mormon and Moroni as they viewed the millions of dead bodies of their people and lamented that they were gone, and there was nothing that could be done about it. All was silent, lifeless, and morbid. This would be the final state of all things had it not been for a Redeemer.

Figure 7

(Birch, *Notes,* after page 174)

What does this figure represent in the world of the Egyptians?

- A seated ithyphallic god with a hawk's tail, holding aloft a flail. This is a form of Min, the god of the regenerative, procreative forces of nature, perhaps combined with Horus, as the hawk's tail would seem to indicate. Before the god is what appears to be a bird presenting him with a Wedjat-eye, the symbol of all good gifts. In other

95

hypocephali, it can also be an ape, a snake, or a hawk-headed snake that is presenting the eye. This figure represents Nehebka, a god and one of the judges of the dead in the 125th chapter of the Book of the Dead. Nehebka was considered to be a provider of life and nourishment and, as such, was often shown presenting a pair of jars or a Wedjat-eye. As for the bird found in Facsimile 2, this could symbolize the Ba or soul, which the Egyptians often represented as a bird, presenting the Wedjat-eye to the seated god (Rhodes, *The Joseph Smith Hypocephalus,* 11).

• Min is called "the god of the lifted hand" or arm and is shown as a composite of the gods Min and Horus. Min represents the idea of father as an "arc-type parent of all the Kings of Egypt" (Nibley, *Abraham in Egypt,* 200). Horus is represented by the hawk-back, extending over the back of the throne, and is the principle of priesthood and kingship verifying the king's rightful place on the throne (Nibley, *The Message of the Joseph Smith Papyri,* 198; *Abraham in Egypt,* 203). Above the lifted hand is the flail scepter, which represents "power to beget or create and sustain life" (Nibley, *Abraham in Egypt,* 141–42). Note that Min does not grasp the scepter, for his arm and hand must be extended completely as representing the sign of the cubit (the distance from the elbow to the tip of the middle finger), for in his role as Horus (Re-Harakhti), he is Lord of Maat (truth) (Morenz, *Egyptian Religion,* 129).

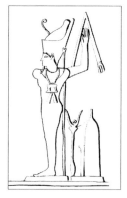

(Budge, *The Gods of the Egyptians,* 2:27)

(Keel, *The Symbolism,* 286)

Osiris in the character of Min, god of the lifted arm (Budge, *Osiris and the Egyptian Resurrection,* 1:21).

The cubit is the sign of Maat, and he is also shown standing on that sign. He wears the crown of Upper and Lower Egypt. The name Min means Holy of Holies (Mercer, *An Egyptian Grammar,* 161). The two tall feathers of Amon derive from Min (Bleeker, *Hathor and Thoth,* 58). "Thou art the beautiful Prince, who risest like the sun with the white crown, and thou art the Lord of radiant light and the creator of brilliant rays" (Budge, *The Gods of the Egyptians,* 2:8).

(Keel, *The Symbolism,* 287)

- Min-Amon. A distinguishing feature is the "long bar which descends to the ground from the back of his head (crown) and seems intended to prevent him from falling." He wears the headdress of Amon (Rawlinson, *History of Ancient Egypt,* 1:332).

- This Min figure represents both the god and the deceased; he is both giving a commitment and, in return, receiving divine powers and attributes (Harris, *The Facsimilies of the Book of Abraham,* 72).

- In front of the god Min-Horus in Figure 7 is a curious symbol. It seems to be a ka sign into which has been fused three jackal heads.

 = +

(Budge, *An Egyptian Hieroglyphic Dictionary,* 2:782b; 1:182a)

One hieroglyphic dictionary shows the *ka* sign with one jackal head merged into it.
Our figure has three.

The ka is a word that relates to vital strength and is used to refer to "the intelligence, essential nature, or life-force of the deceased" (Harris, "The Book of Abraham Facsimilies," 253). When the ka sign has three strokes beside it, indicating that it is to be emphasized

 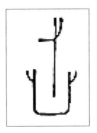 

three times, the word ka becomes kau, which signifies "words of power" (Budge, *An Egyptian Hieroglyphic Dictionary,* 2:783a).

The sign of the jackal head is titled *useru,* which means "to be strong, to be mighty" (Budge, *An Egyptian Hieroglyphic Dictionary,* 1:181b–82a). When occurring three times, *Useru* means mighty powers (Budge, *An Egyptian Hieroglyphic Dictionary,* 1:182a) and is seen as a "badge or insignia of might or potency" (Erman, *Wörterbuch,* 1:363).

  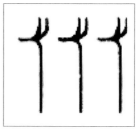

The jackal is used as a determinative in the concepts of "a guide, the god Anubis, judge, chief, master, chief judge, wisdom, time," (Budge, *An Egyptian Hieroglyphic Dictionary,* 2:588a and b). The god Anubis is "he who is over the secrets" (Gardiner, *Egyptian Grammar,* 459) and one of his names—Ap-uat or Wepwawet (Brodrick, *A Concise Dictionary of Egyptian Archaeology,* 19)—means literally "the opener of the ways." His office was to introduce the souls of the departed into the divine hidden land (ibid., 23). With these insights, the triple-jackal sign seems to represent the idea of the way being opened to the secrets of the mighty powers of judgment, which are filled with wisdom and associated with time. Time, of course, has three dimensions: past, present, and future.

When both kau and Useru are fused or melted together in this composite sign, it would seem to represent the secrets of the words of power, mighty in judgment and wisdom that open the way into the dimensions of eternity.

What meaning is given to this figure by the Prophet Joseph Smith or Abraham?

- "Represents God sitting upon his throne, revealing through the heavens the grand Key-words of the Priesthood; as, also, the sign of the Holy Ghost unto Abraham, in the form of a dove"

(Explanation: Figure 7).

If we look at this Egyptian figure as an imitation, what gospel principles can we see in it?

- The god Min on the throne, with the tail of a hawk, speaks to the principle of descending and ascending. This is a principle that relates both to God and to man (Nibley, *Abraham in Egypt,* 199). In the principle of descending, God is represented as revealing through the heavens, power, covenants, and key words to save His children. In the principle of ascending, it relates to the initiate (Adam, Abraham, or any to whom the priesthood has come) possessing those same powers, covenants, and key words as they are revealed by the Holy Ghost.

The Holy Ghost, in the sign of the dove, is holding out the eye of Horus, which represents a fulness of all things, to the initiate. Interesting that he has arms! Doves do not have arms. The bird is stylized with arms in the sign of the ka. The ka is the symbol of embrace. Both the ka and the eye are symbols for words of power. "Together they show the principle of giving and receiving a fulness of all things, coupled with the idea of embracing" (Gardiner, *Egyptian Grammar,* 453).

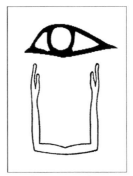

Words of power (Budge, *An Egyptian Hieroglyphic Dictionary,* 2:783, a and b).

A passage in the Pyramid Texts says, "O Atum-Khoprer [Adam, the Ancient of Days (Nibley, *Abraham in Egypt,* 215)] you set your arms about them as the arms of a ka-symbol, that your essence might be in them. O Atum, set your arms about the king . . . as the arms of a ka-symbol, that the king's essence may be in it, enduring for ever"

(Faulkner, *The Ancient Egyptian Pyramid Texts*, 246).

- As was mentioned above, the Min character is portrayed in a pro-creative manner. This is not an attempt to be indecent but to teach a principle. We see the arm to the square (the sign of a covenant) on a man portrayed with power to be a *father*. The Lord said to Noah, "But with thee will I establish my *covenant,* even as I have sworn unto thy father, Enoch, that of thy poster-ity shall come all nations" (JST Genesis 8:23). Here we see that by *covenant,* Noah is to be a *father.* The Lord made the same promise to the sons of Noah, and then he made a significant additional promise:

> And God spake unto Noah, and to his sons with him, saying, And I, behold, I will establish my *covenant* with you, which I made unto your father Enoch, con-cerning your seed after you. . . . And the bow shall be in the cloud; and I will look upon it, that I may remember the everlasting *covenant,* which I made unto thy father Enoch; that, when men should keep all my command-ments, Zion should again come on the earth, the city of Enoch which I have caught up unto myself. And this is mine everlasting *covenant,* that when thy posterity shall embrace the truth, and look upward, then shall Zion look downward, and all the heavens shall shake with gladness, and the earth shall tremble with joy; And the general assembly of the church of the firstborn shall come down out of heaven, and possess the earth, and shall have place until the end come. And this is mine everlasting *covenant,* which I made with thy father Enoch. (JST Genesis 9:15, 21–23; emphasis added)

Of course, this covenant was first made with Adam. "This is why Adam blessed his posterity; he wanted to bring them into the pres-ence of God. They looked for a city ['whose builder and maker is God.' (Hebrews 11:10.)]" (Smith, *Teachings,* 159). We will visit this theme again when we study the rim of our facsimile.

- It is especially interesting that the god Amon is shown with a crown that has behind it a, "long bar which descends to the ground from the back of his head (crown), and seems intended to prevent him from falling" (Rawlinson, *History of Ancient Egypt,* 1:332). We might think about this a long time before we could see a gospel principle in it; however, there is a likeness. The crown is the Deseret-Crown. It is a flat, circular cap that represents the sun with tall feathers on the top, representing the two truths. The bar is holding up the crown. It is heavy. Why is it heavy? The scriptures help us see the symbolism. Speaking of those who do not qualify for eternal glory, the Lord says that they must minister to "those who are worthy of a far more, and an exceeding, and an eternal weight of glory" (D&C 132:16). The word weight in this instance refers to the intensity of the light. The bar suggests that the light or glory of the crown is weighty, indeed.

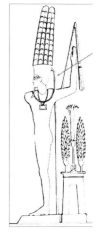

Figures 8–11

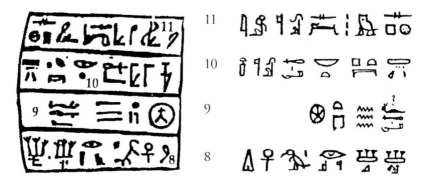

What does this block of text mean in the world of the Egyptians?

- This text is a prayer to the god Djabty (mentioned on the rim) who is Osiris (Rhodes, *The Joseph Smith Hypocephalus*, 4).

  Line 11: Oh God of the Sleeping Ones from the time of the Creation.

  Line 10: O Mighty God, Lord of Heaven and Earth, (and)

  Line 9: the hereafter, and his Great Waters.

  Line 8: Grant life to the soul of the Osiris Sheshonk.

- The text of line 8 is most significant, for it is a plea to the Egyptian god to grant life to the soul of a person who had taken upon himself the name Osiris. This makes what is happening a ritual performance. It is an act of granting life to an initiate. The life-sign had rich meaning. The glyphs that make up the name ankh are:

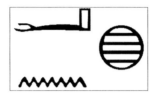

Top left: The hand sign of giving; bottom left: the water sign of washing or cleansing, and (right) the placenta sign of birth and renewal (Gardiner, *Egyptian Grammar,* 508).

- The ankh symbol is best described as "a knot in a sash, with ends hanging down." A visualization of this would be a sash tied around the waist with a knot or bow on one side with the ends hanging down. It represented life because it was a "knotted belly-band or naval string" (Nibley, *The Message of the Joseph Smith Papyri,* 252). Because of the knot, it represented oath or covenant, "for the purpose of the oath is to *bind*—the Egyptian word for oath . . . is simply ankh, originally a 'knot'" (Nibley, *Lehi in the Desert,* 201).

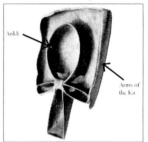

(Aldred, *Egypt to the End,* 57)

An alternate word for bind is to seal or seal up, "the idea being . . . that one swears by one's life, so that if the oath is broken, so likewise 'the cord of life,' i.e., the umbilical cord, is broken" (Nibley, *The Message of the Joseph Smith Papyri,* 252). The ankh is also associated with "the giving of the 'vital fluid,' always (implying) a gift of life. The God embraces him and transmits to him the divine fluid. This exchange is given reciprocally, it is the very foundation of the Egyptian cult: ceaselessly the king offers to the god and receives from him the gift of life in all the rites of the sacred service" (Nibley, *The Message of the Joseph Smith Papyri,* 252).

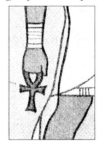

(Budge, *The Gods of the Egyptians,* 2:59)

When shown another way, the symbol is held in the hand and thus becomes a key (Sety, *Abydos: Holy City of Ancient Egypt,* 135). The shape of the figure itself suggests a "sun-figure depicting disk, sky, and rays" (Nibley, *The Message of the Joseph Smith Papyri,* 252, 153). It is the idea of ascension to the horizon (veil), through which one could enter into the eternal realm or sphere of the gods. The kings in their inscriptions, elongated this upper circle and made a cartouche in which they wrote their sacred king-names, signifying that they were knotted or tied into the realm of the gods, "to all that which is encircled by the sun" (Gardiner, *Egyptian Grammar,* 74). Hence, it is a symbol of "life which remains to one even after death" (Brodrick, *A Concise Dictionary of Egyptian Archaeology,* 14). As a representation of

Cartouche (Gilbert, *Treasures,* frontispiece)

eternal life (Gardiner, *Egyptian Grammar,* 557), "ankh is life in the highest sense, being a total of air, breath of life, light and health" (Nibley, *The Message of the Joseph Smith Papyri,* 142).

In the text of Figure 8, the god is asked to grant ankh to the soul of the Osiris Shishaq (Sheshonq). The name in this formula-text represented the person who had taken upon himself the name Osiris in much the same way that one would take upon himself the name of Christ. The name Shishaq is a name of one of the pharaohs of the XXI dynasty (Rhodes, *The Joseph Smith Hypocephalus,* 5) and may be the one who plundered Solomon's temple (see 2 Chronicles 12:9).

The god Osiris is giving Ankh to the king (Patrick, *All Colour,* 52).

It is curious that this name should be here. Such a name found in this setting may have been ritual in nature, for it is possible that it refers more to the pharaonic office of kingship than to a specific person. The name Shishaq is associated with the ideas of appointing, commanding (Gardiner, *Egyptian Grammar,* 480), ordaining, ordering, predestining or assigning (Faulkner, *A Concise Dictionary of Middle Egyptian,* 260–61), fixing, deciding, determining, allotting, designing, decreeing, commissioning, authorizing, and something decreed or ordained by God (Budge, *An Egyptian Hieroglyphic Dictionary,* 2:722b).

What meaning is given to this text by the Prophet Joseph Smith or Abraham?

- Figure 8. "Contains writings that cannot be revealed unto the world, but is to be had in the holy temple of God."
- Figure 9. "Ought not to be revealed at the present time."
- Figure 10. "Also."
- Figure 11. "Also. If the world can find out these numbers, so let it be. Amen" (Explanation: Figure 8–11).

If we look at this Egyptian text as an imitation, what gospel principles can we see in it?

- God of the "sleeping ones." The scriptures say of the dead that "their sleeping dust was to be restored unto its perfect frame" (D&C 138:17).
- God is called the "Mighty God" thirteen times in the scriptures.
- God is "Lord of heaven and earth" (Acts 17:24).
- The hereafter is the place of departed spirits, where "the spirits of all men, whether they be good or evil, are taken home to that God who gave them life" (Alma 40:11).
- "And I, God, made . . . the great waters under the firmament" (Moses 2:7).
- The text of Figure 8 centers on the idea of God granting eternal life through sacred ordinances to those who have taken upon them his name. These concepts are illuminated in the following scriptures and quotes:

  "I will magnify my *name* upon all those who receive and abide in my law" (D&C 132:64; emphasis added).

"And may the Spirit of the Lord be poured out upon you; and may he *grant unto you eternal life"* (Mosiah 18:13; emphasis added).

"And if you do this, behold I *grant unto you eternal life,* even if you should be slain" (D&C 5:22; emphasis added)

"I will clothe him with thy robe, and strengthen him with thy girdle, and I will commit thy government into his hand: . . . And the *key* of the house of David will I lay upon his shoulder; so he shall open, and none shall shut; and he shall shut, and none shall open" (Isaiah 22:21–22; emphasis added).

"The power and authority of the higher, or Melchizedek Priesthood, is to *hold the keys* of all the spiritual blessings of the church" (D&C 107:18; emphasis added).

"All those who receive the priesthood, receive this *oath and covenant* of my Father" (D&C 84:40; emphasis added).

"Incline your ear, and come unto me: hear, and *your soul shall live;* and I will make an everlasting *covenant* with you" (Isaiah 55:3; emphasis added).

"If a man would attain to the *keys* of the kingdom of an *endless life;* he must sacrifice all things" (Burton, "Discourses of the Prophet Joseph Smith," 49–50).

"Love the name of the Lord . . . and *taketh hold of my covenant"* (Isaiah 56:6; emphasis added).

"I *covenant* with thee that thou shalt have *eternal life;* and thou shalt . . . go forth in my *name"* (Mosiah 26:20; emphasis added).

"I will perform the *oath* which I sware unto Abraham" (Genesis 26:3; emphasis added).

The Prophet Joseph Smith speaking of Melchizedek said that he "had power and authority . . . holding the *key* and the power of *endless life"* (Burton, *Discourses of the Prophet Joseph Smith,* 49; emphasis added). And finally, symbolized by the cartouche, we find "his paths are straight, and his *course is one eternal round"* (Alma 37:12; emphasis added).

Figures 12–15

Note: The following figure was severely damaged. Part of it (12) is unreadable; part (13–15) was reconstructed by the Prophet and will be considered later. Only the lower left area is translated below.

 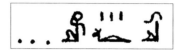

What does this block of text represent in the world of the Egyptians?

- The white text area says, "His [the god's] words" (Budge, *An Egyptian Hieroglyphic Dictionary,* 1:240b).

What meaning is given to this text by the Prophet Joseph Smith or Abraham?

- Figures 12–15: "Will be given in the own due time of the Lord" (Explanation: Figures 12–21).

If we look at this Egyptian figure as an imitation, what gospel principles can we see in it?

- Many other hypocephali have readable text in this area, but for the purposes of this study we will not consider them. For a translation of the readable text in this figure, see page 123.

Figures 16–17
(Note: This block of text is read from upside down and from right to left.)

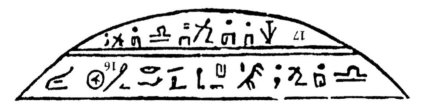

What does this block of text represent in the world of the Egyptians?

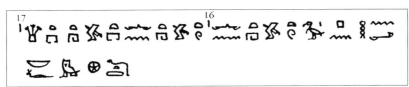

- "May this tomb never be desecrated, and may this soul and its possessor never be desecrated in the Netherworld" (Rhodes, *The Joseph Smith Hypocephalus,* 5).
- The illusion to the idea of a soul possibly being desecrated in the netherworld (the world of spirits) may associate with the need for the Sons of Horus to faithfully watch over the dust of the body so that it will come forth whole in a resurrection. Also, that the spirit on its journey through the netherworld will not be hindered or stopped along the way. A similar plea is written on the hypocephalus belonging to Sir Henry Meux Bart: "I am one of the spirits who came forth from the underworld: grant thou unto me the things which my body needeth, and heaven for my soul, and a hidden place for my mummy. May the god, who himself is hidden, and whose face is concealed who shineth upon the world in his forms of existence, and in the underworld, grant that my soul may live for ever! May the great god in his disk give his rays in the underworld of Heliopolis! Grant thou unto me an entrance and an exit in the underworld without let or hindrance" (Budge, *Egyptian Magic,* 119–20).

What meaning is given to this text by the Prophet Joseph Smith or Abraham?

- Figures 16–17: "Will be given in the own due time of the Lord" (Explanation: Figure 12–21).

If we look at this Egyptian figure as an imitation, what gospel principles can we see in it?

- This plea of protection for the place of burial puts us in mind of the need for dedicating a grave by the priesthood. It also alludes to the constant need for protection by him "who controllest and subjectest the devil, and the dark and benighted dominion of Sheol (hell)" (D&C 121:4).

Figure 18

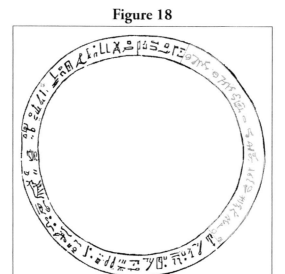

Note: The gray portion of this figure was damaged and was reconstituted by the Prophet Joseph Smith.

What does this figure and its text represent in the world of the Egyptians?

Edge:

• "I am Djabty in the House of the Benben in Heliopolis, so exalted and glorious. [I am] a procreative bull without equal. [I am] that Mighty God in the House of the Benben in Heliopolis . . . that Mighty God" (Rhodes, "A Translation and Commentary," 265).

• This is a statement by the God *Djabty* (Osiris) (Rhodes, *The Joseph Smith Hypocephalus,* 4), who dwells in the *Benben* (Holy of Holies) (Keel, *The Symbolism of the Biblical World,* 167) of the temple in *Heliopolis* (the heavenly Heliopolis, in the same sense as the heavenly Jerusalem) (Rhodes, *The Joseph Smith Hypocephalus,* 13), declaring that he is exalted and glorious, a procreative *bull* (sire or father) without equal, the "Mighty God" (name given to Osiris) (Rhodes, *The Joseph Smith Hypocephalus,* 4).

- The name Djabty is an abbreviation for the more complete Djeba Demdj (Nibley, "One Eternal Round," Lecture 1), which combines the meaning supply, furnish, equip, provide, give something in the place of something else, restore, replace, indemnify, pay for, discharge a debt or obligation, reward, clothe, etc., with uniting, totaling, all in all, altogether, summation, joining, associating, assembling, bring together, reassembling a dismembered body, accumulating, compiling, extending, etc. (Budge, *An Egyptian Hieroglyphic Dictionary,* 2:904–6, 880b; see also Gardiner, *Egyptian Grammar,* 514; Faulkner, *A Concise Dictionary of Middle Egyptian,* 313). This shows the great benevolence and encompassing power of this god.

What meaning is given to this figure and text by the Prophet Joseph Smith or Abraham?

- Figure 18: "Will be given in the own due time of the Lord" (Explanation: Figures 12–21).

If we look at this Egyptian figure and text as an imitation, what gospel principles can we see in it?

- The rim translation speaks of the great city of Heliopolis; in fact it is mentioned three times. There was an earthly and a heavenly city of Heliopolis. Jewish tradition maintains that Abraham taught the priests of Heliopolis astronomy and other sciences (Rhodes, *The Joseph Smith Hypocephalus,* 5). As mentioned, the word Heliopolis is a Greek rendering, with helio meaning light and polis meaning city. It was called the city of the Sun. Other hypocephali in the area where ours was damaged expand the notion of this city and its temple. From the Leyden hypocephalus, we read, "O Djabty in the house of Benben so exalted and glorious; a copulating bull, that great and mighty god, in the temple of the grand old man in Heliopolis. Come to the Osiris, (name of the person), grant thou that she become like one among thy followers. She is a god, who is in the temple of the grand old man in Heliopolis" (Nibley, "One Eternal Round," Lecture 3).

With the background we now have, we could give a rendering of this in our own words: O God in the holy of holies of the temple, praise to thee, who is exalted and glorious, the father of all men, the great and mighty God, in the temple of the holy city, venerating Adam, the ancient of days; please come hither, as I am an initiate, and grant that I become like one among thy followers, I am becoming as a god, through the temple of the ancient of days.

Another hypocephalus says, "I have come forth from the underworld with Ra from the House of the Great Aged One in Heliopolis" (Budge, *Egyptian Magic*, 119–20).

I cannot stress too much that the temple in Heliopolis was that of "the grand old man." This was Atum, the Ancient of days, or Adam (Nibley, *Abraham in Egypt*, 215). This has reference to the Egyptian imitation of Adam being the principal character in temple worship from the foundation of the world, and that he is the one who leads his posterity through the ordinances. Joseph Smith said that the Lord "set the ordinances to be the same forever and ever, and set Adam to watch over them, to reveal them from heaven to man, or to send angels to reveal them" (Smith, *Teachings*, 168.) The point I want to make here is that there is a connection between this information and the fact that Adam and his posterity looked for a city.

In our discussion of Figure 7, we spoke of the covenant made with Adam and his posterity that the great city of Zion would come down out of heaven and join with the earthly city. The Lord said that he would "gather out mine elect from the four quarters of the earth, unto a place which I shall prepare, an Holy City, that my people may gird up their loins, and be looking forth for the time of my coming; for there shall be my tabernacle, and it shall be called Zion, a New Jerusalem. And the Lord said unto Enoch: Then shalt thou and all thy city meet them there, and we will receive them into our bosom, and they shall see us, and we will fall upon their necks, and they shall fall upon our necks, and we will kiss each other" (Moses 7:62–63).

In light of all this, the symbol for Heliopolis—a pillar or column with a tenon on top—is most instructive (Gardiner, *Egyptian Grammar*, 495). A tenon is an extension made on the top of a pillar to fit into a corresponding cavity or mortise in the bottom of another pillar that makes a close and secure joint when they are fitted together.

Annu (Budge, *The Egyptian Book of the Dead,* cxxxiii)

iwn, heliopolis

The full rendering of the name Heliopolis as shown above includes a pillar, a vase, and a crossroads sign in a circle. The pillar is called a "light tower" and the "house of the sun" (Budge, *The Egyptian Book of the Dead,* cxxxiii-cxxxiv; Gardiner, *Egyptian Grammar,* 495). The bowl or vase represents the goddess Nut, who is the symbol of the holy city and the "bosom" of god (Gardiner, *Egyptian Grammar,* 530). The final sign is that of a city with crossroads. It represents the idea of gathering from the four quarters of the earth to a central meeting place (Gardiner, *Egyptian Grammar,* 498). Since there was the idea of both an earthly and a heavenly Heliopolis, we can see in these symbols the representation of the joining of these two cities in one.

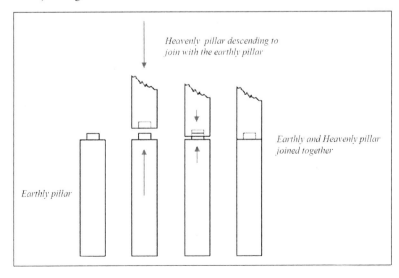

Figures 19–21

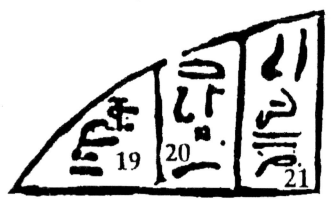

What does this block of text represent in the world of the Egyptians?

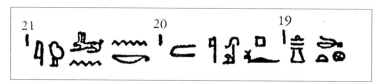

- You will be as that God, the Busirian (Osiris). Busiris was a cult center of Osiris in the Delta and was thus used as an epithet of Osiris (Rhodes, *The Joseph Smith Hypocephalus,* 5).
- This is a promise to the person for whom the Hypocephalus was made that he would become as Osiris. One text speaking of these things says, "Stand up, and sit thou upon the throne of Osiris," and "beautiful and great are these things which thy father Osiris hath done for thee. He hath given thee his throne" (Budge, *Osiris and the Egyptian Resurrection,* 2:333, 358).
- One document says, "(Osiris) appeared to man not only as the god and judge of the dead, but also as the creator of the world and of all things in it. He who was the son of Ra became the equal of his father, and he took his place side by side with him in heaven" (Budge, *Egyptian Ideas of the Future Life,* 61).

What meaning is given to this text by the Prophet Joseph Smith or Abraham?

- Figures 19–21: "Will be given in the own due time of the Lord" (Explanation: Figures 12–21).

If we look at this Egyptian text as an imitation, what gospel principles can we see in it?

- The Savior promises that those who are faithful to him "shall have fulness of joy; and ye shall sit down in the kingdom of my Father; yea, your joy shall be full, even as the Father hath given me fulness of joy; and ye shall be even as I am, and I am even as the Father; and the Father and I are one" (3 Nephi 28:10).

- Joseph Smith speaking of the faithful dead, said:

  "Although the earthly tabernacle is laid down and dissolved, they shall rise again to dwell in everlasting burnings in immortal glory . . . (and) they shall be heirs of God and joint heirs with Jesus Christ. What is it? To inherit the same power, the same glory and the same exaltation, until you arrive at the station of a God, and ascend the throne of eternal power, the same as those who have gone before. What did Jesus do? Why, I do the things I saw my Father do when worlds came rolling into existence. My Father worked out his kingdom with fear and trembling, and I must do the same; and when I get my kingdom, I shall present it to my Father, so that he may obtain kingdom upon kingdom, and it will exalt him in glory. He will then take a higher exaltation, and I will take his place, and thereby become exalted myself. So that Jesus treads in the tracks of his Father, and inherits what God did before; and God is thus glorified and exalted in the salvation and exaltation of all his children. It is plain beyond disputation, and you thus learn some of the first principles of the gospel, about which so much hath been said. (Smith, *History of the Church*, 6:306)

- Enoch speaking of his inheritance with Christ, said, "Thou hast made me, and given unto me a right to thy throne, and not of myself, but through thine own grace" (Moses 7:59).

Figures 22–23

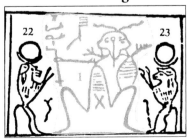
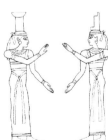

(Wilkinson, *The Complete Gods*, 35)

What do these figures represent in the world of the Egyptians?

- As pointed out eariler, on either side of the god are two apes (numbers 22 and 23) with horned moon-disks on their heads, in an attitude of adoration. There are also two serpents, one on either side of the seated deity. The small serpents are horned vipers in one form or another that appear in most of the hypocephali. This horned viper is of the Cerastes Cornutus variety (Gardiner, *Egyptian Grammar*, 476). The Cerastes is called Sa-ta in Egyptian (Budge, *An Egyptian Hieroglyphic Dictionary*, 2:584b). We get some idea why the Sa-ta-serpent is in this position as we read words spoken by it to a deceased person who coveted its powers: "I am the serpent Sata whose years are many. I die and am born each day. I am the serpent Sata which dwelleth in the uttermost parts of the earth. I die and I am born again, and I renew myself, and I grow young each day" (Budge, *The Gods of the Egyptians*, 2:377).

The Sata was a form of the Uraeus Serpent, a symbol of divinity and royalty, for the walls of the abode of Osiris were surmounted by living Uraei, and the god Ra wore two uraei upon his forhead. Every king is represented with at least one Uraeus upon his forehead. In religious texts, the Uraeus is associated with Isis and Nephthys (Budge, *The Gods of the Egyptians*, 2:377). The two apes in Figure 1 are none other than Isis and Nephthys, hence the Sata serpents are right at home here.

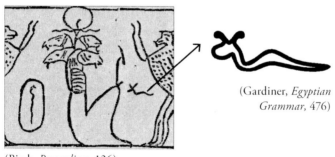

(Gardiner, *Egyptian Grammar*, 476)

(Birch, *Proceedings*, 126)

Isis and Nephthys are described in the following terms:

- The plumes, which are the two eyes on the crown of Min-Horus. The plumes are the going forth of Isis and Nephthys. They "protect and provide what his head lacketh. They are 'eternity' and 'everlastingness.' Eternity is the day, Everlastingness is the night"

(Budge, *The Book of the Dead*, 31–32). Osiris says, "I am the keeper of the volume of the book (the Register or the Tablet of Destiny) of the things which have been made, and of the things which shall be made . . . the things which have been made are Eternity, and the things which shall be made are Everlastingness, and that Eternity is the Day, and Everlastingness the Night" (Budge, *The Book of the Dead*, 379–80).

- The feathers of Isis and Nephthys are emblems of spirit and truth (Nibley, *Lehi in the Desert*, 336).
- The two exceedingly great uraei are upon the head of the god. Their names are Millions of Years and Traverser of Millions of Years and Begetter of Millions of Years (Budge, *The Book of the Dead*, 32–34). They are the two shining spirits (Budge, *An Egyptian Hieroglyphic Dictionary*, 1:24a).
- They who have gone around behind Osiris and embrace him triumphantly in peace and in right and truth (Budge, *The Book of the Dead*, 231–32).
- The nursing mothers who together embrace the king (Nibley, *The Message of the Joseph Smith Papyri*, 105).
- They possess magical powers and Urt-Hekau (mighty one of words of power) (Budge, *The Gods of the Egyptians*, 2:256).
- Two Maat (truth) goddesses. The Egyptians call the extreme limits of the country, their confines and seashores, Nephthys—a name expressly signifying the "end of anything." It is clear that Nephthys is the personification of the darkness and of all that belongs to it, and that her attributes were rather of a passive than active character. She was the opposite of Isis in every respect: Isis symbolized birth, growth, development, and vigor, but Nephthys was the type of death, decay, diminution, and immobility. Isis and Nephthys were, however, associated inseparably with each other, even as were Horus and Set, and in all the important matters that concern the welfare of the deceased, they acted together. Isis represented the part of the world that is visible, while Nephthys represents that which is invisible. We may even regard Isis as the day and Nephthys as the night. Isis and Nephthys represent respectively the things that are and the things that are yet to come into being, the beginning and end, birth and death, and life and death (Budge, *The Gods of the Egyptians*, 2:256–58).

- The two ape goddesses or "the guardians who give judgment" (Rossiter, *The Book of the Dead*, 36–37; Budge, *The Egyptian Book of the Dead*, 51–52).

Of these goddesses, it is said:

- Nephthys was the goddess of the death that was not eternal (Budge, *The Gods of the Egyptians*, 2:258), and although a goddess of death, she was associated with the coming into existence of the life that springs from death. Like Isis, she was a female counterpart of Amsu, the ithyphallic god who was at once the type of virility, reproduction, and regeneration. Isis and Nephthys prepared the funeral bed for their brother Osiris, and together they made the swathings wherewith his body was swathed after death; they assisted at the rising of the sun-god when he rose upon this earth for the first time; they assisted at the resurrection of Osiris; and in all ages, they together aided the deceased to rise to the new life by means of the words which they chanted over his bier (see Budge, *The Gods of the Egyptians*, 2:258–59).
- The deceased is said to breathe the breath of Isis and is declared to be the very son of Isis and her twin sister Nephthys (Budge, *The Gods of the Egyptians*, 2:204). Isis and Nephthys are declared to be the divine daughters of Nut (see Budge, *An Egyptian Hieroglyphic Dictionary*, 2:584a). Of the deceased, the record says, "the arms of Nut who bore you are about you so that your beauty may be upraised" (Faulkner, *The Ancient Egyptian Coffin Texts*, 1:54). Here we have the deceased being the offspring of Isis, Nephthys, and Nut. Because these are principles, we can imagine that Isis and Nephthys are the "arms" of Nut.
- Speech of Isis, "I have granted that thou mightest be as a god" (Budge, *The Egyptian Book of the Dead*, 229). "I am that which is has been, and shall be, and no man has lifted my veil" (Baily, *The Lost Language of Symbolism*, 1:168).
- "Your time yonder is no more . . . O Isis and Nephthys, come together, come together, unite, unite" (Faulkner, *The Ancient Egyptian Pyramid Texts*, 46).
- They are the two pylons at the entrance of every temple (Nibley, *The Message of the Joseph Smith Papyri*, 116).
- Isis and Nephthys are the Maati goddesses, the two truths in the

Hall of the Judgment of Osiris. They are called the twins (Budge, *Osiris and the Egyptian Resurrection*, 2:224). Isis is the wife of Osiris, and Nephthys is the wife of Set. Osiris and Set are twin brothers, as are Horus and Set (twin brothers married to twin sisters) (Budge, *Osiris and the Egyptian Resurrection*, 2:213, 224). They are also called Rekhtti goddesses. The term rekh means to know, to be wise, to be acquainted with (Budge, *An Egyptian Hieroglyphic Dictionary*, 1:430–31; *Osiris and the Egyptian Resurrection*, 2:70). Osiris was said to be arrayed in apparel, which had been specially woven for him by the two Rekhti goddesses (Budge, *The Gods of the Egyptians*, 1:462). The names of Isis and Nephthys are written with the determinative of two eyes (Budge, *An Egyptian Hieroglyphic Dictionary*, 1:431a), and they are "one" (Budge, *The Book of the Dead*, 254).

(Budge, *An Egyptian Hieroglyphic Dictionary*, 2:840b)

- Both Isis and Nephthys as the two truths hold the Uas scepter (Rossiter, *The Book of the Dead*, 63).
- Khnum sits between two cynocephalic (dog-headed) apes, which are Isis and Nephthys.
- The dead says, "I have gone up in Pe to the Souls of Pe, I am girt with the girdle of Horus, I am clad with the garment of Thoth, Isis is before me and Nephthys is behind me, Wepwawet opens the way for me, Shu lifts me up, the Souls of On set up a stairway for me in order to reach Above, and Nūt puts her hand on me just as she did for Osiris on the day when he died" (Faulkner, *The Ancient Egyptian Pyramid Texts*, 180–81).

What meaning is given to these figures by the Prophet Joseph Smith or Abraham?

- Figures 22–23: The stars Kli-flos-is-es or Hah-ko-kau-beam receive light from the revolutions of Kolob. (Note: This description of Figures 22–23 is included in Joseph's explanation of Figure 5.)

If we look at these Egyptian figures as an imitation, what gospel principles can we see in them?

- Here we see two forces that stand on either side of God. They are the two truths, the two eternities, the two eyes, the record or book of things that have been, and will be, made. They are spirit and truth; they represent millions of years. They are the nurturing and nourishing mother-influence. They possess words of power. One is death, the other is life; one is visible, the other is invisible. They are guardians of judgment. They represent the resurrection and relate to the holy environment of God. Their secrets have never been revealed to man. They are the gates to every temple. They are knowledge and wisdom.

  What are they? In short, they are a representation of the mind of God. We see these two goddesses weeping at the bier of Osiris (Faulkner, *The Ancient Egyptian Coffin Texts,* 1:45) and rejoicing at his resurrection. We see them giving homage to all the principles of truth and observing all things as Watchers, for they are truth itself, the two daughters of Maat. They represent the "the past, the present, and the future," which are with God, "one eternal 'now'" (Burton, *Discourses of the Prophet Joseph Smith,* 77). They are the "punishment, which also was eternal as the life of the soul should be, affixed opposite to the plan of happiness" (Alma 42:16). They are the two wings of the hen, pointing to the past and the future, as the Lord says, "How oft have I gathered you," and again "How oft will I gather you as a hen gathereth her chickens under her wings," to nourish you (3 Nephi 10:4, 6). They are perfectly represented in the two cherubims on the ark of the covenant. For the scripture says, "Thou shalt make two cherubims of gold . . . one cherub on the one end, and the other cherub on the other end: even of the mercy seat" (Exodus 25:18–19). We are then told that the Lord "dwelleth between the cherubims" (1 Samuel 4:4), that "he sitteth between the cherubims," (Psalm 99:1), and that he spake from "between the two cherubims" (Numbers 7:89). "Cherub, in Hebrew signifies fulness of knowledge . . . and Moses says, that two cherubims covered the mercy-seat with their wings extended on both sides, and looked one to another, having their faces turned toward the mercy-seat which covered the ark. God is supposed to sit on the mercy-seat whose face the angels in heaven always behold and upon whom their eyes are fixed to observe and receive his commands, and towards Christ, the true Propitiatory which mystery they desire to look into" (Cruden, *Cruden's Unabridged Concordance,* 59; see also Exodus 37:9; Matthew 18:10; 1 Peter 1:12; D&C 77:4).

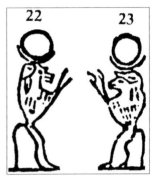

Figure 1

Could there be any better subjects chosen to represent the idea of two stars "receiving light from the revolutions of Kolob," who in turn give that light to the star, Kae-e-vanrash, which in turn gives light to the Sun? (Facsimile 2, explanation figure 5). These stars are portrayed as baboons that are known, as we have seen, for "holding up their hands to receive the first warming rays of the sun after the cold desert night as if worshiping the sun at its rising" (Rhodes, *The Joseph Smith Hypocephalus,* 8). "Both their upraised hands receiving life and light and their double headdresses show . . . the sun-moon dependency" (Nibley, *The Three Facsimilies from the Book of Abraham,* 70), the moon being "established for ever. . . . as a *faithful witness* in heaven" (Psalm 89:37; emphasis added).

In the ancient Egyptian Coffin Texts, an invitation given to the king says, "Isis has summoned you, Nephthys has called you,

(these) spirits are given to you, they come to you bowing. Go to, open the mansion of yon soul. If you find them (Isis and Nephthys) playing, you shall sit down between them" (Faulkner, *The Ancient Egyptian Coffin Texts,* 1:59). The idea is that the king is to go to the temple and find the place where Isis (all eternity future) and Nephthys (all eternity past) are "playing." The Egyptian word hab translated here as playing has the alternate meanings of combined, joined, united, or embraced (Budge, *An Egyptian Hieroglyphics Dictionary,* 1:467a). It is accompanied with the sign of the two goddesses reaching out their hands to touch each other. The altar of marriage is the place in the temple that is set between the two eternities (attested by the mirrors on both sides) where a couple may be joined or united or sealed not only for eternity but also into the two eternities.

Just as Ra in Figure 3 has taken up his position between Isis and Nephthys (the two eyes who face each other), God has taken His place upon His throne "in the bosom of eternity" (D&C 88:13).

Figure 3

Important considerations

1. The Reconstruction

As we have shown in our discussion of Figures 12–15 and 18 above, there was considerable damage to Facsimile No. 2 at some time in its history. There is evidence to show that the damage predated its coming into the hands of Joseph Smith. We do not know much about Joseph's work with the damaged parts, except what we can surmise from a comparison of the ink drawing found with the Joseph Smith Egyptian Alphabet and Gramma, and the published version. Near the publishing date for Facsimile No. 2, Joseph recorded in his journal a meeting with the engraver: "At my office exhibiting the Book of Abraham in the original to Brother Reuben Hedlock, so that he might take the size of the several plates or cuts, and prepare the blocks for the Times and Seasons; and also gave instruction concerning the arrangement of the writing on the large cut, illustrating the principles of astronomy, with other general business" (Smith, *History of the Church,* 4:543). The idea of arranging suggests that materials were at that time being crafted into the areas that were damaged.

(Ashment, *The Facsimilies*, 39)

A side-by-side comparison of the ink drawing from *Joseph Smith's Egyptian Alphabet and Grammar,* and the published product.

In comparing the ink drawing found with *Joseph Smith's Egyptian Alphabet and Grammar*, which some believe is a hand-drawing of what Facsimile 2 looked like in the original, with the published version, we get some idea of what Joseph may have been talking about. Careful researchers have suggested that the areas on the facsimile that have been filled in came from other manuscripts in the possession of the prophet that were part of the Book of Abraham package.

The area of Figure 3 in Facsimile 2 has a connection with a similar figure in the Framed ("Trinity") papyrus. The missing texts in Figures 13–15 and 18 seem to have been supplied from the Small "Sensen" text, lines 2–4 (also called the "Book of Breathings") ("Background of the Church Historian's Fragment," *Improvement Era*, February 1968, 40D, 40I; Rhodes, *The Joseph Smith Hypocephalus*, 2).

The regular text of Facsimile No. 2 is called Book Hand Egyptian and consists of hieroglyphic signs that are, in these days, quite familiar to most of us. They read in our facsimile from right to left. However, the glyphs chosen by Joseph from the Sensen text to fill in the damaged area of the rim and the missing text of boxes 13–15 is hieratic, which is a hieroglyphic shorthand. This text was inserted upside down to the other text and in such a way that it reads from left to right (Rhodes, *The Joseph Smith Hypocephalus*, 2). Joseph gave no explanation for this. In fact, other than the small journal entry quoted above, there is no mention of damage, an ink drawing, a reconstruction, or a borrowing of material from other texts. This has all been discovered by examination.

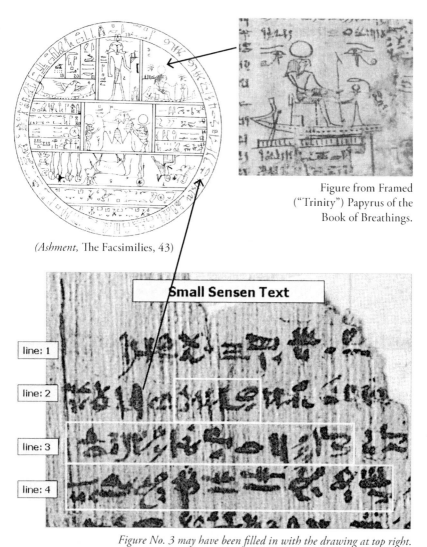

(Ashment, The Facsimilies, 43)

Figure from Framed
("Trinity") Papyrus of the
Book of Breathings.

Figure No. 3 may have been filled in with the drawing at top right.

Figure 12–15 and 18 were filled in from line 2-4 of the Sensen text. It is not known from where or how the other areas were reconstructed.

One thing is certain. Joseph's translation and explanations deal only with the figures. He did not offer any explanation of the text areas. When Facsimile No. 2 was ready for publication, he made this critical statement about the text in the document (Figures 8–21): "Will be given in the own due time of the Lord." This implies that what was done and how it was done will one day be known, and it will be by the same power and inspiration that the initial translation was done. The next statement implies that

Joseph knew a lot more than he was saying, and the Lord, whose work this is, had given some cautions about saying too much. "The above translation is given as far as we have any right to give at the present time."

The curved cutaway of facsimile two (below right) shows the hieratic text that Joseph placed. The area with the hieroglyphs is the hieratic text converted to regular bookhand Egyptian. Below that is a translation.

"Khebyt, Khebyt, . . . his two arms upon his breast, being as wrapped like a book, the Book of Breathings, being written according to what is" (Nibley, *The Message*, 20).

The name Khebyt is part of the name of the owner of the Sensen text, and it is repeated twice in this inscription. The root khb means "to carry away" (Budge, *An Egyptian Hieroglyphic Dictionary,* 1:538). If we translate the whole rim, together with what can be read in figures 13–15, this is how it might read:

> I am Djabty in the House of Benben in Heliopolis, so exalted and glorious. I am a virile bull without equal. I am that Mighty God in the House of the Benben in Heliopolis. . . . [Carry away, carry away, (in the) two arms upon his breast, being as wrapped . . . the Book of Breathings, being written according-to-what is] his words, that Mighty God in Heliopolis.

Some have supposed that this material is simply filler. However, the Book of Breathings, which was with the Abraham papyri, had the same general purpose as the hypocephalus. Copies were placed with the dead for the same reason. We could surmise that after the initiate had learned the grand truths from the great God Djabty, who is in the House of Benben in Heliopolis, which words could be written either on a Hypocephalus or in a Book of Breathings, he was to secret them away, holding them close to his heart wrapped in his arms, for they contained a knowledge of things as they really are. After all, was it not within the enclosed arms of an Egyptian mummy that these sacred records came into the hands of Joseph Smith? (Todd, *The Saga of the Book of Abraham*, 115, 134, 158).

2. A Hierarchy of Planets and Stars

- Following is a chart showing an idea of the arrangement of the stars and planets as given in the explanations to Facsimile 2:

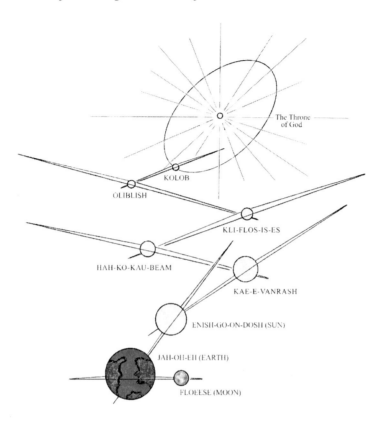

- Of the order of planets presented in Facsimile No. 2, Elder Parley P. Pratt once wrote, "When we contemplate the majesty of the works of God as unfolded in all the simplicity of truth, opening to our view the wide expanse of the universe, and showing the laws and regulations, the times and revolutions of all worlds, from the celestial throne of heaven's kings, or the mighty Kolob, whose daily revolution is a thousand years, down through all the gradations of existence to our puny earth, we are lost in astonishment and admiration" (Hunter, *Pearl of Great Price Commentary*, 35).
- The scriptures speak of the Lord's relationship to the planets and stars: "He telleth the number of the stars; he calleth them all by their names" (Psalm 147:4). "Lift up your eyes on high, and

behold who hath created these things, that bringeth out their host by number: he calleth them all by names by the greatness of his might, for that he is strong in power; not one faileth" (Isaiah 40:26). "Mine hand also hath laid the foundation of the earth, and my right hand hath spanned the heavens: when I call unto them, they stand up together" (Isaiah 48:13).

- In the panoramic view opened by the Prophet Joseph, we see a hierarchy of planets, one planet giving light to the one below while receiving light from the one above. This is reminiscent of our priesthood line of authority, and makes one wonder if, in the cosmic order of things, the Lord, through His prophet, has given us our earth's "light-line" of authority back to Kolob and to His throne.

3. The Journey of Salvation

- We asked in an earlier part of this study if Facsimile No. 2 might represent the journey that man must take in "following the Son." Every part of this document relates to light and power, risings and settings, comings and goings, death and resurrection, hierarchal chains of bodies of light, and keys and powers that are passed up and down for governments. Let us look at this document again with that in mind.

It has been observed that "the main circle in the center, is always divided into two equal or nearly equal opposing parts, usually upside-down to each other and sometimes facing each other, the one representing the orbs of light in the upper heavens, the other 'the lower regions'" (Nibley, *The Three Facsimiles of the Book of Abraham,* 14–15).

There is a visible flow and transmission of power from the highest realms of the gods to the lowest regions of the earth and back again. This flow follows in the order of Figures 1, 2, 3, 7, 5, 6, and

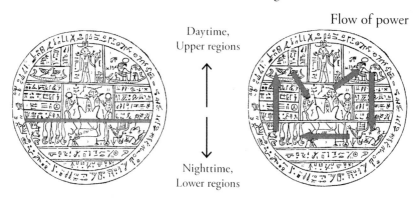

Daytime,
Upper regions

Flow of power

Nighttime,
Lower regions

4, returning again back to 1. It is a circular power train of life.
- We will take the facsimile apart and lay the figures out on a flat surface in order to see the flow.

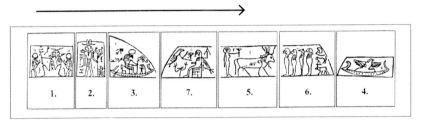

- Figure 1 represents God in the center of the universe with all power and knowledge.
- Figure 2 represents the Son of God opening the way to put the creative plans of the Father into effect. Through the Atonement that He will perform, He holds the keys to all things.
- Figure 3 represents the Savior going forth as Creator; He is a transporter of life throughout the universe
- Figure 7 represents Adam in the Garden of Eden after this world had been created. He is receiving the keys and powers through the Holy Ghost. At this point Adam falls from the garden and the earth falls also. Brigham Young explains, "the earth was framed . . . near the throne of our Father in heaven. And when man fell . . . the earth fell into space, and took up its abode in this planetary system, and the sun became our light. When the Lord said— 'Let there be light,' there was light, for the earth was brought near the sun that it might reflect upon it so as to give us light by day, and the moon to give us light by night" (in *Journal of Discourses,* 17:143; see also Abraham 5:13).
- Figure 5 represents the idea that the earth after the fall has need of the sun for its light. We see power being given to the sun to begin its work in relationship to the fallen earth.
- Figure 6 represents the earth in its four quarters. The figures also represent all men on the face thereof. Behind the earth is represented the animal and plant kingdoms. All these things feed on each other. They all deteriorate and eventually die. This is the lowest point of the power or light chain.
- Figure 4 represents the moment of glorious resurrection where all things are reclaimed from death. Resurrection enables man to

return to the presence of God, and hence the cycle returns to Figure 1.

- It is easy to see the temple journey in these various stations of our facsimile. (Compare the following information with Talmage, *The House of the Lord*, 152–68.)

1	2	3	4	5
Divine Power Center	*Creative Power*	*Garden of Eden*	*The Earth where we live and die*	*Resurrection*
(Celestial)	*(Creation)*	*(Terrestrial)*	*(Telestial)*	*(Terrestrial)*

- Station 1—The celestial kingdom. But in this case it can represent, as the divine center, the baptismal font signifying the Atonement of Christ, which is the center axis of eternity around which all things revolve and the bedrock upon which all things rest. The initiate must pass through the gate of the waters of baptism to begin the journey into the eternities.
- Station 2—Leaving the font, the initiate enters the creation room. Here he views the creation of earth and all things on the face of it.
- Station 3—The initiate views Adam, who was one of the gods and had helped form the earth, and Eve, his wife, being placed in the garden. The earth is in a terrestrial state. Adam and Eve partake of the forbidden fruit, which requires that they leave the garden. However, before they go, they make covenants with God and obtain from Him grand key words of the Holy Priesthood, which, we learn, were "revealed to Adam in the Garden of Eden" (Facsimile 2: Figure 3).
- Station 4—As Adam and Eve fall from the garden, they enter the lone and dreary world, or the telestial kingdom. It is here where all things live and die.
- Station 5—The journey proceeds to the terrestrial world where things are taught that are necessary to pass through the veil into the presence of God. Thus prepared, the initiate passes through into the celestial kingdom, which returns man back to the divine center from which he came.
- We read much about the hypocephalus relating to the journey of the sun across the sky. If we were to place the elements of Facsimile 2 on

the bearings of the compass, we would see that the temple journey indeed follows the sun across the sky. We have used the Alberta temple floor plan as a basis for this concept. The journey begins at the lowest level of the temple—at the font (marked No. 1 on the drawing). This is the center of eternity and marks the Atonement upon which all things rest, and the center axis around which all things rotate. The journey proceeds to the room of creation, which is in the east (No. 2), the place of the rising sun. It then proceeds to the south (No. 3), following the sun in its noonday journey, then to the west (No. 4) where all things, like the going down of the sun, shrivel and die. Next it goes to the north (No. 5), representing new life and resurrection, before heading back to the south (No. 6) into the presence of God from which all things came in the beginning, This is where the sun is at its highest point in the center of the sky. Hence in the journey, the candidate literally "follow[s] the [Sun] Son, with full purpose of heart" (2 Nephi 31:13). The initiate is the living lotus flower, always open to the sun, drawing upon its warmth and life. A joyful initiate in the Book of the Dead, speaking of what went on in the Divine House, said, "The Great God looketh upon thee, and he leadeth thee along the path of Happiness" (Budge, *The Book of the Dead*, 630).

• Did Joseph's understanding of the arrangement of the figures in Facsimile No. 2 inspire him as he set up the "true and ancient order" for the first time in this dispensation, in the red-brick store in Nauvoo, hanging canvasses to represent the various stages of the endowment?

> In the "Red Brick" store (the first place where temple ordinances were administered), the large open upper floor of the store was set up as Joseph envisioned the interior of a temple should be. Using canvas, he had the room parti-tioned into several sections representing the stages of man's progression from his creation to his future possible place in the celestial kingdom. He engaged Shadrach Roundy, Noah Rogers, Dimick B. Huntington, Daniel Carns, and Lucius N. Scovil on 3 and 4 May 1842 to help arrange the room preparatory to giving the endowments. Scovil later testified that "We . . . went to work making the neces-sary preparations, and everything was arranged represent-ing the interior of a temple as much as the circumstances

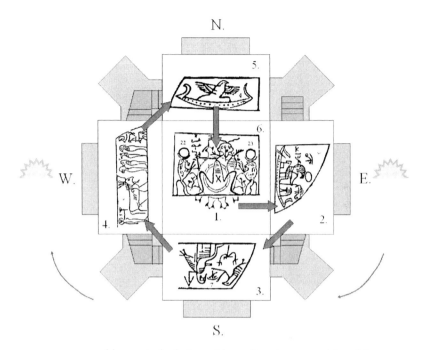

would permit, he being with us dictating everything. He gave us many items that were very interesting to us, which sank with deep weight upon my mind, especially after the temple was finished at Nauvoo and I had received the ordinances. . . . I can and do testify that I know of a surety that room was fitted up by his order which we finished in the forenoon of the said 4th of May 1842." (Letter of Lucius N. Scovil to the Editor, Deseret News Semi-Weekly, 15 February 1884, p. 2.). (Ehat, "They Might Have Known," *BYU Studies* 19, no. 2, 166)

When we think of all the things that Facsimile No. 2 inspires, and the rich and deep meaning it contains, most of which can only be understood after initiation in the temple, we marvel that the Lord gave us such an incredible document in the infancy of the Church. Though it is in our scriptures, it is generally ignored and almost completely unexplored. We are much like Lehi who "arose in the morning, and went forth to the tent door, and to his great astonishment he beheld . . . a round ball of curious workmanship" (1 Nephi 16:10). In a way that's what happens to us when we open the Book of Abraham to Facsimile No. 2.

We might wonder how Lehi learned to use this round ball. "The Lord said unto him: Look upon the ball, and behold the things which are written" (1 Nephi 16:26). Have we ever done that? We all know that the ball was called Liahona. That word is composed of three parts: L, which in Hebrew means to; iah, which is an abbreviated form of the name Jehovah; and ona, or on, which we discussed earlier in this chapter, means light, a meaning derived from the idea of the great Egyptian city of light—Heliopolis (Ludlow, *A Companion to Your Study of the Book of Mormon,* 1:129). Liahona means to Jehovah is light.

The word Heliopolis is included three times around the rim of our facsimile. It makes us wonder if there is some kind of message here. Is Facsimile 2 a sort of compass for us? Are there some pointers in it, and does it contain directions? It makes you wonder if the Lord had some leaning toward this document in our scriptures when He said, "I will instruct thee and teach thee in the way which thou shalt go: I will *guide* thee with mine *eye"* (Psalm 32:8; emphasis added).

As a parting thought, I conclude with this scripture: "For what doth it profit a man if a gift [for instance, Facsimile No. 2] is bestowed upon him, and he receive not the gift? Behold, he rejoices not in that which is given unto him, neither rejoices in him who is the giver of the gift" (D&C 88:33).

CHAPTER 5

Facsimile No. 3: Abraham on the Throne

What would a document of this nature represent in the world of the Egyptians?

• This scene shows a man (Figure 5), his hand raised in adoration and a cone of perfumed grease and a lotus flower on his head (ancient Egyptian festival attire), being introduced by Maat (Figure 4), the goddess of justice, and Anubis (Figure 6) the guide of the dead, into the presence of Osiris (1), who is enthroned as king of the netherworld, or the spirit world. Behind Osiris stands Isis (Figure 2), and in front of him is an offering stand (Figure 3) with a jug and some lotus flowers on it. Over the whole scene is a canopy with stars painted on it to represent the sky (Baer, *The Breathing Permit of Hôr,* 126).

- Osiris wears the Atef crown and holds the scepters of his office, which are the flail and the crook (Griffiths, *The Origins of Osiris and His Cult,* 85–88).

- After our discussion of the temple nature of Facsimile No. 2, it shouldn't surprise us to find documents that actually portray the process of coming into the presence of Osiris. Some of them are more elaborate than others. Ours is one of the simpler ones.

(Rossiter, *The Book of the Dead,* 82–83)

We can see in the above judgment scene from the Book of the Dead (The papyrus of Hunifer, circa 1320 B.C., No. 3, "The Weighing of the Heart"), the initiate (on the left) being led by Anubis toward the place of judgment. Anubis has the Ankh symbol in his hand showing that he has the keys and the power, and that what is being done is relating to rebirth and eternal life. The candidate is wearing brilliant white clothing. Next the heart of the deceased is being weighed on the scales against the feather of Maat (Truth), with Thoth recording the outcome.

In the next scene, having passed the judgment, the candidate is brought to a partition by Horus, who again holds the keys, and petitions Osiris to let him come into his presence. Osiris sits enthroned in a sacred shrine flanked by two pillars with a wrapped cloth, symbolizing that the entrance into his presence is based on the principle of wrapping or enfolding or embracing (the veil) (Hornung, *Conceptions of God,* 34–39). The throne sits on the Maat stone of truth, upon which sits the sign of great waters (space) out of which is growing a lotus flower holding the four canopic gods. These symbolize the coming forth of all things from Osiris and that he is Lord of all the earth. Behind him stand Isis and Nephthys, the two eyes of eternity representing the mind of Osiris as comprehending all things from eternity to eternity, raising their hands in veneration. The top of the shrine is lined with fiery Uraeus serpents, or flame-spitters, who guard the person of Osiris, and to the front of him is the marvelous Eye of Horus that represents the fulness and completeness of resurrection and glory. Above the procession is a small replica of the candidate giving homage to all the major gods of Egypt, symbolizing he has kept all the laws and regulations that are specified by the principles that these gods represent. The offering table before him represents his offerings and sacrifices.

What meaning is given to this document by the Prophet Joseph Smith or Abraham?

- The Prophet Joseph captions this document: "Abraham is reasoning upon the principles of Astronomy, in the king's court" (Explanation: Facsimile 3).

If we look at this Egyptian document as an imitation, what gospel principles can we see in it?

- Once we see the big picture in the more elaborate scenes, it is easier to understand the more abbreviated ones. Facsimile No. 3 shows the candidate flanked by Anubis (the holder of keys and powers) and led by Maat (Truth) into the presence of Osiris (God). Behind Osiris is Isis who, as a lone figure, personifies the throne (Bonwick, *Egyptian Belief and Modern Thought,* 144), and with her sister, Nephthys, the two truths of eternity. In her right hand, she holds the Ankh symbol of covenant and new birth; her left hand is raised in veneration. Osiris has truth before him and truth behind him. He wears the crown of truth, sits on the throne of truth, and speaks forth the words of truth, and the lotus flower is before him bearing witness that he is the light.

Figure 1

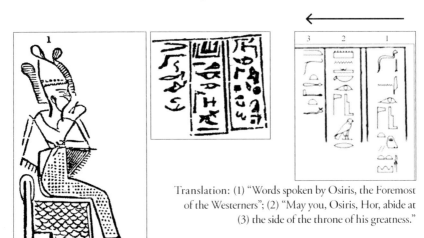

Translation: (1) "Words spoken by Osiris, the Foremost of the Westerners"; (2) "May you, Osiris, Hor, abide at (3) the side of the throne of his greatness."

What does this figure represent in the world of the Egyptians?

- This is the great god Osiris. He is the god of the resurrection and the judge of the dead (Brodrick, *A Concise Dictionary of Egyptian Archaeology,* 121). His crown is the two-plumed Atef, a symbol of power, priesthood, light, and holiness (Harris, *The Facsimilies of the Book of Abraham,* 47).

  It is "the white two-feathered supreme crown of heavenly authority." Both the whiteness and the feathers are symbolic of the heavenly light that burst upon the world at the coronation, the "luminous" quality of the one who mounts the throne. The two feathers are both the well-known Maat-feathers, "feathers of truth," symbolic of light that passes between the worlds.

The Atef crown is "the oldest and holiest of Pharaoh's many crowns. The two big feathers on it are emblems of spirit and truth, the symbols of Shu, the oldest and most 'spiritual' of the gods, and of Maat, who is truth itself" (Nibley, *Lehi in the Desert,* 336). "Osiris causes brilliance to stream forth through the two feathers. He is the leader of the gods . . . who commands the Great Council (in heaven)" (Nibley, *Abraham in*

Egypt, 141–42). The scepters carried by Osiris are the flail and the shepherd's crook, for he is the good shepherd who cares for the flock. He must also prod them and at times drive them with his flail. The crook and the flail are symbols of mercy and justice and are instruments of rescue and punishment respectively (Harris, *The Facsimiles of the Book of Abraham,* 47). The flail and crook are "symbolic of the power that created, being the whip of light or power, bestirring all things to life and action" (Nibley, *Abraham in Egypt,* 142).

Osiris, sitting on the throne, was dressed in a tightly fitting robe of feathers, symbolic of righteousness (Hamlyn, *Egyptian Mythology,* 144). The feathers on both Osiris and the side of the throne are a representation of Horus (light) and Maat (truth) (Watterson, *The Gods of Ancient Egypt,* 60, 107).

- Osiris wears the White Crown of Upper Egypt. In shape, this crown resembles the sun (the bulb at the top) shedding its rays over the head of the wearer. To this was attached two Maat feathers, symbols of the two truths, or the two eyes (Isis and Nephthys), making this crown identical, in principle, with that worn by Ra in the throne-boat. This crown of Osiris was called atef.

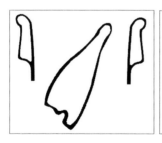  

- Sometimes the atef crown was depicted as the bowl of the lotus plant. As we learned earlier, the lotus plant bursts its seed out of the top of the pod. The depiction, below, shows the sun as the *seed* being burst out of the top of the crown of Osiris (Bonwick, *Egyptian Belief and Modern Thoguht,* 243). This is the same symbolism that we saw in Facsimile 2, Figure 5, where the Lady of the Wadjet eye was holding a lotus over the loins of the cow (sun) symbolizing that the cow (sun) was the seed bursting forth from the lotus.

(Budge, *Osiris and the Egyptian Resurrection,* 1:338)

(Nibley, *Abraham in Egypt,* 142–43).

- The crook and flail scepters (above) held by Osiris designate justice and judgment as well as the office of both priesthood and kingship

What meaning is given to this figure by the Prophet Joseph Smith or Abraham?

- "Abraham sitting upon Pharaoh's throne, by the politeness of the king, with a crown upon his head, representing the Priesthood, as emblematical of the grand Presidency in Heaven; with the scepter of justice and judgment in his hand" (Explanation: Figure 1).

If we look at this Egyptian figure as an imitation, what gospel principles can we see in it?

- We have said much about Osiris, but there is one thing more to say. On two occasions in Church history, those associated with the Prophet Joseph gave us an insight into him. Joseph received two papyrus rolls with the mummies. One was written by Father Abraham and the other by his great-grandson Joseph, who was sold into Egypt. The Prophet said, "I commenced the translation of some of the characters or hieroglyphics, and much to our joy found that one of the rolls contained the writings of Abraham, another the writings of Joseph of Egypt" (Smith, *History of the Church,* 2:236). Oliver Cowdery

(Nibley, "Background of the Church Historian's Fragment," *Improvement Era,* February 1968, 40b)

writing to William Frye about the Egyptian manuscripts described some of the things that were on the papyrus of Joseph. "The inner end of the same roll (Joseph's record), presents a representation of the judgment: At one view you behold the Savior seated upon his throne, crowned, holding the scepters of righteousness and power" (Hunter, *Pearl of Great Price Commenary*, 36–37).

The papyrus (bottom of previous page) is the representation he is describing and the person on the throne is none other than Osiris.

On another occasion, the Reverend Henry Caswall visited Nauvoo. He describes being led into the office of Joseph Smith, President of the Church of Latter Day Saints, where he was shown the Egyptian curiosities. The person who addressed him showed him the same document mentioned above and said, "Mr. Smith informs us that this picture is an emblem of redemption. Do you see those four little figures? Well, those are the four quarters of the earth," and "that (referring to the person sitting on the throne) is Jesus Christ keeping the devil from devouring the four quarters of the earth" (Todd, *The Saga of the Book of Abraham*, 236–37). The point here is that the Prophet Joseph Smith had taught his associates the connections and associations in these documents. They knew that Osiris on the throne in some way related to Jesus Christ.

• Since the Prophet Joseph specifically mentions the crown, we should say a few more words about that. As we said, the crown of Osiris was called the atef crown.

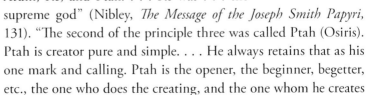

In the gods of the Egyptian drama of creation and resurrection, a pattern of three is consistently followed. They are a "trinity of Atum, Re, and Ptah. . . . Re was . . . the supreme god" (Nibley, *The Message of the Joseph Smith Papyri*, 131). "The second of the principle three was called Ptah (Osiris). Ptah is creator pure and simple. . . . He always retains that as his one mark and calling. Ptah is the opener, the beginner, begetter, etc., the one who does the creating, and the one whom he creates is Atum" (Nibley, *The Message of the Joseph Smith Papyri,* 134). It is hard in some of these associations to avoid hearing the name of Adam for that of Atum, noting how closely Atum resembles Adam in his attributes.

The name Atum signified both the Creator and "the collective sum of all future beings" as well as "all-embracing," "the Sum of everything," or the uniting of many in one, of combining all premortal beings in a single archetype who thereby represents all beings hereafter. He is "the Ancient One" par excellence . . . the Word of Ptah incarnate" (Nibley, *The Message of the Joseph Smith Papyri,* 133). "All the high gods who participate in this scene are thought of as real persons having strictly human form, for all their divinity" (Nibley, *The Message of the Joseph Smith Papyri,* 135). The Sensaos breathing text begins: "I am Re in his rising; I am Atum in his setting." This takes us back to the oldest Egyptian creation Drama. The creation is taking place at sunrise, the dawning of a new day but in the middle of the sunrise brought about by Re, there is a sunset brought about by Atum. The mystery is solved when we discover that one of the creators (Atum) is coming down to earth. "The human drama is here being depicted. Atum is unique as one who is a creator, yet human. Equally at home in heaven or on earth. The texts tell of Ra coming down in the evening in the 'cool of the day' to 'walk with Atum.' Atum is placed by Re in a 'Garden of Reeds' and placed in charge of the plants of which he freely eats" (Nibley, *The Message of the Joseph Smith Papyri,* 132–33).

The reason for this treatise on the creator gods is because Joseph Smith said the crown of Osiris is "emblematical of the Grand presidency in heaven." We have identified three creator gods: Ra, Ptah, and Atum. Ra the supreme god can be associated with God the Father, Ptah as the Opener of the Way, and the actual creator can be associated with God the Son, remembering that he is the preexistent Osiris, and Atum is, of course, the Ancient of Days—Adam. But what are we to think? There is no mention here of the Holy Ghost, and the Holy Ghost is the third member of the Godhead. Elder Mark E. Peterson of the Quorum of the Twelve once spoke on this subject, saying, "Brigham Young taught that Adam, or Michael, assisted the Deity in the creation of the world. He said, 'It is true that the earth was organized by three distinct characters, namely, Elohim, Yahovah, and Michael, these three forming a quorum.' Then he distinguished these three from the Holy Trinity, as he spoke in the same paragraph defining 'the Deity, as Father, Son, and Holy Ghost'" (in *Journal of Discourses,* 1:51).

"It therefore becomes clear beyond all question that the three who organized the earth were a separate quorum, a different triumvirate, apart from the Holy Trinity. The entire Trinity is identified by President Young as Deity, but not so with the group that organized the earth, for one of them, Michael, was not Deity—he was still an angel, although the head of the angels" (Peterson, *Adam, Who Is He?* 83–84).

In other words, when the Father and the Son made plans to create the earth, they had need of a specialized creator (Adam) to act with them, one who was not a member of the Godhead. Therefore, they organized themselves into a presidency to form the earth. Joseph Smith refers to them not as the Grand Presidency of Heaven but the Grand Presidency in Heaven. In other words, it was necessary to organize in heaven a presidency to form the earth. The Grand Presidency of Heaven was already in existence.

This all comes together when we read a declaration of Osiris (Ptah) in the Coffin Texts who says, "So says Osiris. You shall see me in my great Atef-crowns which Ra gave to me and which Atum . . . made firm for me" (Faulkner, *The Ancient Egyptian Coffin Texts,* 1:233).

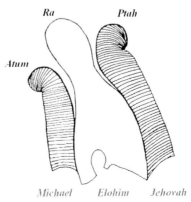

Here, in very fact, is a Grand Presidency in Heaven represented by the Atef crown.

I now break from the typical way that I have been presenting these figures to a discussion about Abraham, as he takes the throne of Pharaoh to do what the Lord sent him there to do—teach the Egyptians about the creations of God. (Note: The remainder of the Egyptian characters will be treated as the discussion unfolds.)

I have made much of the idea that the facsimiles were used in some way to tell Abraham's story, or at the very least as templates into which the story of Abraham has been crafted. Facsimile No. 3 is a template for understanding the account of Abraham's sitting on the throne of Pharaoh and teaching his people.

One account says Abraham "sat upon the throne by Pharaoh's permission, and all the court brought their children to be instructed in the principles of astronomy." The pharaoh "had 365 of the highest nobles of the land come with their children to Abraham to sit on the throne and be taught the principles of astronomy by Abraham." "He began his preaching, 'Blessed be God who created the sun, the moon, and the planets'" (Nibley, *Ancient Documents and the Pearl of Great Price,* Lecture 23, 11).

We will now pick up an imaginary conversation:

Q. Why use Egyptian characters to tell the story of Abraham?

Q. Let me first ask you a question. According to the Prophet Joseph Smith, what is the theme of this document?

A. Abraham reasoning upon the principles of astronomy in the king's court.

Q. How did he get there?

A. I'm not sure.

A. We know from our study of Facsimile 1 that Abraham was a rival of the king. Both claimed to hold the priesthood powers of heaven. However, during the renewal festival rites, Abraham's claim was verified by the Lord. Abraham gives us the account:

> They . . . endeavored to take away my life by the hand of the priest . . . of Pharaoh. . .
>
> And it came to pass that the priests laid violence upon me, that they might slay me . . . upon this altar . . .
>
> And as they lifted up their hands upon me, that they might

offer me up and take away my life, behold, I lifted up my voice
unto the Lord my God, and the Lord hearkened and heard,
and he filled me with the vision of the Almighty, and the angel
of his presence stood by me, and immediately unloosed my
bands . . .

And the Lord broke down the altar . . . and smote the priest
that he died; and there was great mourning . . . in the court of
Pharaoh. (Abraham 1:7, 12, 15, 20)

Q. I would think he would be angry. Why would the king mourn?

A. The renewal festival was not a rite of vengeance but of an earnest
determination to obtain the true priesthood. When Abraham could not
be sacrificed, the king was greatly disappointed, but his disappointment
seems to have turned to admiration.

Q. How do we know that?

A. By his willingness to admit Abraham into his court and listen to
his teachings.

Q. Is that so strange?

A. For a pharaoh it was. We have to understand that an Egyptian
pharaoh was a god to his people. His words and actions were infallible.
To admit Abraham into his presence and be instructed by him was an
incredible concession.

Q. I still don't see the relationship between Abraham and Osiris.

A. Let's consider a scenario. Let's assume for a moment that Facsimile
No. 3 was an after-the-fact record. Imagine an unknown Egyptian artist-
scribe trying to record an account of Abraham's visit to the court of Pharaoh. Abraham is in a very interesting position. The pharaoh, in profound
respect, has stepped aside to let him sit upon his throne.

Q. Why would he be allowed to sit on the throne?

A. The throne of Pharaoh was seen as the seat of perfect judgment
and absolute truth. Pharaoh was quick to realize that the priesthood
and power of Abraham was superior to his own. By letting Abraham
instruct from the throne, the king was announcing that his words were
the truth! With Abraham in that position, the artist-scribe would be
hard pressed to say enough good about him. His logic may have gone
as follows:

• This man has the priesthood.
• He has not been able to be put to death.
• He has been received into the presence of the king.

- He is now sitting on the king's throne.
- If he is sitting on the king's throne, he must be greater than the king.
- If he is greater than the king, he must be a god.
- There is only one god who has power over death—Osiris!

Q. I see. So it could be an artist-scribe who is using the figure of Osiris to teach us the magnitude of Abraham?

A. It's a possibility, and for all we know, a scribe in that position might have believed that Abraham really was Osiris.

Q. The pharaoh (Figure 2) and the prince of pharaoh (Figure 4) certainly look like women, but they are identifiable Egyptian goddesses. What is going on?

A. The artist-scribe would be in a real predicament here. Abraham had been invited into the court of Pharaoh, and the pharaoh in awe and wonder has placed Abraham on his own throne. We don't know all the reasons why he did that. It may well be that he was willing to trade his throne for the true priesthood (Nibley, *Abraham in Egypt*, 133).

Q. But that wouldn't have worked would it? His lineage would have prevented it.

A. Yes, that is true. Nonetheless, the artist-scribe faces the responsibility of drawing Abraham on the throne with the king's crown on his head and holding his scepters. Now the problem. How does he draw the king? He can't be portrayed off his throne, for that would discredit him. He can't be on the throne, for it is occupied. We can see that he settled the matter in the only acceptable Egyptian fashion.

Q. What was that?

A. A disguise (Nibley, *Abraham in Egypt*, 133).

Q. A disguise? So Figure 2 could be Pharaoh in disguise?

A. And what a clever one. Isis was not a real person but a ritual one. The pharaohs became kings through their mothers, and she was the representation of that matriarchal ascent to the throne (Hart, *A Dictionary of Egyptian Gods and Goddesses*, 101). Her name Isis is written with a hieroglyphic throne, and she was regarded as the personification of the throne itself (Watterson, *The Gods of Ancient Egypt*, 89; Tobin, *Theological Principles of Egyptian Religion*, 45). She was also regarded as the mother or bearer of the king, and he is sometimes depicted sitting on her lap attesting to his divine kingship as her son, who is sitting upon the throne (Frankfurt, *Ancient Egyptian Religion*, 6–7). Seeing the pharaoh in this disguise

*Translation:
"The great Isis,
mother of the
god."*

(Frankfort, *Ancient
Egyptian Religion*,
frontispiece)

could bear no stronger message that he is literally on the throne.

Q. So Pharaoh is in the disguise of Isis, which tells us that though he is not shown on the throne, he still occupies it. Why does Isis have her hand raised?

A. Her raised hand tells us that Pharaoh, whom she represents, is giving honor to the person on the throne.

Q. The same principle must exist with Figure 4. The Prophet Joseph says that it is "the prince of Pharaoh," but I believe you said that it is Maat. Who is she?

A. She is another ritual woman, and the prince or son of Pharaoh in this case must be portrayed as a woman, for he is not the son of the king shown on the throne but of the king in disguise. Thus we find a systematic harmony in these characters.

Q. Isn't Maat a word for truth?

A. She was the embodiment of all truth, order, justice, law, and righteousness. She represented things as they really are (Hart, A *Dictionary of Egyptian Gods and Goddesses*, 116–17). It is more than coincidence that she is used in this instance, for by using her, the artist-scribe is indicating that what is going on is legal, right, and according to divine justice and is acceptable in preserving the dignity of the king while at the same time giving honor to Abraham. Her hand is also raised toward him in honor.

(Translation:
"Maat,
lady of the
west.")

Q. Who are the other characters?

A. The Prophet Joseph tells us that one

is "Shulem, one of the king's principal waiters," and the other is "a slave belonging to the prince" (Explanation: Figures 5–6).

Q. Why a waiter and a slave in the king's court at a time like this?

A. Let's not forget why the pharaoh wanted Abraham to sit on his throne in the first place—to teach. And we know that the Lord sent Abraham to Egypt for that very purpose (see Abraham 3:15). If we think back to the birth of Christ, it was not enough for the Father to reveal it to wise men; he wanted the poor as well as the rich, the humble as well as the proud to know. He therefore sent His angels to the shepherds. It was not long before the news was common knowledge throughout the land.

Q. So these two could represent the idea that all classes of people were to hear the words of Abraham.

A. I think that is what the stars above their heads represent. The idea connects back to the four canopic gods in Facsimile No. 1 (Nibley, *Abraham in Egypt*, 148). Everyone under heaven was to hear Abraham's message. The Egyptian pharaoh was the greatest ruling power in the whole world, and it was from his very throne, through Abraham, that the words of life were to go forth. At least that is one way to look at it.

As we come to the close of this chapter, it is necessary to say a word about Shulem.

The Prophet Joseph says that Shulem was "one of the king's principal waiters." We think of a waiter as a server of food, but waiter in this instance is more like "an Intendent of the palace" (Nibley, *Abraham in Egypt*, 147) or a supervisor over the business of the palace; note that he is one of the principal ones.

Research has found that documents like Facsimile No. 3 have patterns, and the constant in most all of them is that the person who is being led into the presence of the God, generally by Maat, is the owner of the document (Nibley, *Abraham in Egypt*, 146). In other words, the document in the first instance was made because of an experience had by the person.

"But why Shulem? He plays no part in the story of Abraham. His name never appears elsewhere. He simply pops up and then disappears. Yet he is the center of attention in facsimile No. 3. That is just the point: these palace servants would in their biographical Stelae glorify the moment of their greatest splendor for the edification of their posterirty every after. Facsimile No. 3 may well be a copy on Papyrus of the funeral stele of one Shulem who memorialized an occasion when he was introduced to an illustrious Canaanite in the palace of the king. This would be the one sure means of guaranteeing a preservation of Abraham's story in Egypt. Shulem is the useful transmitter and timely witness who confirms for us the story of Abraham in the Court of Pharaoh" (Nibley, *Abraham in Egypt*, 147).

The name Shulem has a connection with the Hebrew prime root shalam, forming the basis of words in the Old Testament such as Shulamite, of the Song of Solomon 6:13, and shulam, shelam, and shalem (Strong, *Strong's Exhaustive Concordance of the Bible*, 113, word 7759; 117, words 7999–8004). The word has a variety of meanings but all center in the idea of being reliable, to be a finisher, to sacrifice voluntarily, being full of thanks, and friendly. What more could a king want in a principal waiter. And it is possible that it was more a title than a given name, for the similar *Shulamite* was the "pet name of Solomon's Queen" (ibid.).

Looking again at the scene of Facsimile No. 3, it is as if everything is frozen. All things have ceased; everything is on hold. For what? For the word and the message of Abraham! All things point to him or lead to him. Every foot is in midstride toward him. All faces are toward him, except Maat who is bidding and leading the others to him. All have arms stretched toward him. Even the Lotus flower, which follows the light of the sun across the sky, is open to him. The stars above are witness of him. Can we also put ourselves on hold and be prepared to hear his message? If so, what is his message? Here is his message:

> And, finding there was greater happiness and peace and rest
> for me, I sought for the blessings of the fathers, and the right
> whereunto I should be ordained to administer the same; having

been myself a follower of righteousness, desiring also to be one who possessed great knowledge, and to be a greater follower of righteousness, and to possess a greater knowledge, and to be a father of many nations, a prince of peace, and desiring to receive instructions, and to keep the commandments of God, I became a rightful heir, a High Priest, holding the right belonging to the fathers.

It was conferred upon me from the fathers; it came down from the fathers, from the beginning of time, yea, even from the beginning, or before the foundation of the earth, down to the present time, even the right of the firstborn, or the first man, who is Adam, or first father, through the fathers unto me.

I sought for mine appointment unto the Priesthood according to the appointment of God unto the fathers concerning the seed. (Abraham 1:2–4)

Because the Lord is concerned about all His children, He "hath sent his holy prophets among all the children of men, to declare these things to every kindred, nation, and tongue, that thereby whosoever should believe that Christ should come, the same might receive remission of their sins, and rejoice with exceedingly great joy, even as though he had already come among them" (Mosiah 3:13).

To extend that blessing to the Egyptians, the Savior gave a divine commission to Abraham, "Yea, and behold, Abraham saw of his coming, and was filled with gladness and did rejoice." Abraham and "many before [his] days" were "called by the order of God; yea, even after the order of his Son; and this that it should be shown unto the people, a great many thousand years before his coming, that even redemption should come unto them" (Helaman 8:17–18).

That commission is the message of Facsimile No. 3.

SUMMARY

As we come to the end of this small work on the facsimiles, we are struck with the magnitude of the message and the example of Abraham. How grateful we should be for him! Not only did he preserve and hand down his records, many of which have been translated by the Prophet Joseph Smith, but he also gave us a key for the understanding of the whole world of Egyptian theology—that they were an earnest imitation of the true and ancient order of the Son of God. The explanations of the Prophet Joseph, together with that key, has helped in our journey of learning about the facsimiles.

The second realization is what the facsimiles say after our major study is over and we look at them, almost in farewell. Because they are on separate pages in our scriptures, we might not realize that they fit together. If we put them side by side and look at them again, a message suddenly emerges and we wonder why we haven't seen it before. The message is sequential and underlines the entire plan of salvation.

They resonate:

1. The necessity of sacrifice

The necessity of sacrifice.   The gift of seeing.

The promise of kingship.

2. The gift of seeing
3. The promise of kingship

These three principles are at the heart of every aspect of the gospel and follow a natural sequence. Those who sacrifice for the truth of Christ have the windows of heaven opened to them. They are able to see and comprehend, by the power of the Holy Ghost, things which are reserved for their glory in the presence of God. This process and these things are represented by the Eye.

It is not an accident that the All-Seeing Eye is inscribed on the holy temple of God in Salt Lake City. It represents not only the eye with which God sees us but also the eye He places in us, through the ordinances, so that we can see Him. Through sacred covenants in the temple, we obtain the promises of becoming like God in the worlds to come—even kings and priests, to rule and reign with Him in eternity and, to use scriptural language, we will "obtain . . . the crown over the kingdom of our God" (D&C 76:79).

1. The necessity of sacrifice
   - "And ye shall offer for a sacrifice unto me a broken heart and a contrite spirit. And whoso cometh unto me with a broken heart and a contrite spirit, him will I baptize with fire and with the Holy Ghost" (3 Nephi 9:20).
   - "I have seen your sacrifices in obedience to that which I have told you. Go, therefore, and I make a way for your escape, as I accepted the offering of Abraham of his son Isaac" (D&C 132:50).
   - "All among them who . . . are willing to observe their covenants by sacrifice—yea, every sacrifice which I, the Lord, shall command—they are accepted of me" (D&C 97:8).

2. The gift of seeing
   - "By the power of the Spirit our eyes were opened and our understandings were enlightened, so as to see and understand the things of God" (D&C 76:12).
   - "Let him that is ignorant learn wisdom by humbling himself and calling upon the Lord his God, that his eyes may be opened that he may see" (D&C 136:32).
   - "If ye will enter in by the way, and receive the Holy Ghost, it will show unto you all things what ye should do" (2 Nephi 32:5).
   - "And if your eye be single to my glory, your whole bodies shall be filled with light, and there shall be no darkness in you; and that body which is filled with light comprehendeth all things" (D&C 88:67).

3. The promise of kingship
   - "They shall receive a crown in the mansions of my Father" (D&C 59:2), "a crown of glory that

149

fadeth not away" (1 Peter 5:4), "a crown of immortality, and eternal life" (D&C 81:6). "Come up unto the crown prepared for you, and be made rulers over many kingdoms" (D&C 78:15).

• "Thy scepter [shall be] an unchanging scepter of righteousness and truth; and thy dominion shall be an everlasting dominion, and without compulsory means it shall flow unto thee forever and ever" (D&C 121:46).

• "To him that overcometh will I grant to sit with me in my throne, even as I also overcame, and am set down with my Father in his throne" (Revelation 3:21).

We see that in all three of these areas, Abraham is our exemplar in leading us to Christ.

1. The necessity of sacrifice
    • The sacrifice required of Abraham "shows that if a man would attain to the keys of the kingdom of an endless life; he must sacrifice all things" (Smith, *Teachings,* 322).

2. The gift of seeing
    • "And he said unto me: My son, my son (and his hand was stretched out), behold I will show you all these. And he put his hand upon mine eyes, and I saw those things which his hands had made, which were many; and they multiplied before mine eyes, and I could not see the end thereof" (Abraham 3:12).
    • "And the Lord said unto me: Now, Abraham . . . behold thine eyes see it; it is given unto thee to know" (Abraham 3:6).

3. The promise of kingship
    • "Abraham . . . as Isaac also and Jacob did none other things than that which they were commanded; and because they did none other things than that which they were commanded, they have entered into their exaltation, according to the promises, and sit upon thrones, and are not angels but are gods" (D&C 132:37).
    • "For I am the Lord thy God, and will be with thee even unto the end of the world, and through all eternity; for verily I seal upon you your exaltation, and prepare a

throne for you in the kingdom of my Father, with Abraham your father" (D&C 132:49).

Significantly, the Lord says to each of us: "Go ye, therefore, and do
the works of Abraham; enter ye into my law and ye shall be saved" (D&C
132:32).

SOURCES

Aldred, Cyril. *Egypt to the End of the Old Kingdom*. New York: McGraw Hill Book, 1965.

———. *The Egyptians*. London: Thames and Hudson, 1987.

Ashment, Edward H. "The Facsimiles of the Book of Abraham: A Reappraisal." *Sunstone* 4, nos. 5–6 (1980): 33–48.

Baer, Klaus. "The Breathing Permit of Hôr." *Dialogue* 3, no. 3 (Autumn 1968).

Baily, Harold. *The Lost Language of Symbolism*. 2 vols. London: Ernest Benn Limited, 1957.

Birch, Samuel. "Notes." *Archaeologia* 36 (1855).

———. *Proceedings of the Society of Biblical Archaeology*. 40 vols. London: The Offices of the Society, 1884.

Bleeker, C. J. *Hathor and Thoth*. Leiden, The Netherlands: E. J. Brill, 1973.

Bonwick, James. *Egyptian Belief and Modern Thought*. Indian Hills, Colo.: Falcon's Wing Press, 1956.

Breasted, J. H. *The Development of Religion and Thought in Ancient Egypt.* New York: Charles Scribner's Sons, 1912.

Brodrick, M., and A. A. Morton. *A Concise Dictionary of Egyptian Archaeology.* Chicago: Ares Publishers, 1924.

Budge, E. A. Wallis. *An Egyptian Hieroglyphic Dictionary.* 2 vols. New York: Dover Publications, 1978.

———. *The Book of the Dead.* New York: Bell Publishing Company, 1960.

———. *The Egyptian Book of the Dead.* New York: Dover Publications, 1967.

———. *The Book of the Kings of Egypt.* London: Kegan Paul, Trench, Trubner and Co., 1908.

———. *Egyptian Ideas of the Future Life.* London: Kegan Paul, Trench Trubner and Co., 1899.

———. *Egyptian Magic.* New York: Dover Publications, 1971.

———. *From Fetish to God in Ancient Egypt.* New York: Benjamin Blom, 1972.

———. *The Gods of the Egyptians.* 2 vols. New York: Dover Publications, 1969.

———. *Osiris and the Egyptian Resurrection.* 2 vols. New York: Dover Publications, 1973.

Burton, Alma. *Discourses of the Prophet Joseph Smith.* Salt Lake City: Deseret Book, 1977.

Bush, C. Dana. *Compact Guide to Wildflowers of the Rockies.* Edmonton, Alberta, Canada: Lone Pine Publishing, 1990.

Chart of Egyptian Hieroglyphs. The Royal Ontario Museum, Toronto, Ontario, Canada 1978.

Cook, Melvin A., and M. Garfield Cook. *Science and Mormonism.* Salt Lake City: Deseret Book, 1968.

Cruden, Alexander. *Cruden's Unabridged Concordance to the Old and New Testaments and the Apocrypah.* Old Tappan, N.J.: Flemming H. Revell Co., 1969.

DeBuck, Adriaan. *The Egyptian Coffin Texts.* 7 vols. Chicago: The University of Chicago Press, 1935.

Draper, Richard D., S. Kent Brown, and Michael D. Rhodes. *The Pearl of Great Price: A Verse-by-Verse Commentary.* Salt Lake City: Deseret Book, 2005.

Ehat, Andrew F. "Joseph Smith's Introduction of Temple Ordinances and the 1844 Mormon Succession Question." Master's thesis, Brigham Young University, December 1982.

———. "They Might Have Known That He Was Not a Fallen Prophet—The Nauvoo Journal of Joseph Fielding." *BYU Studies* 19, no. 2 (Winter 1979).

Erman, Adolf, and Hermann Grapow. *Wörterbuch der Ägyptischen Sprache.* 5 vols. Berlin: Akademie-Verlag, 1982.

———. *Life in Ancient Egypt.* New York: Dover Publications, 1971.

Faulkner, R. O. *The Ancient Egyptian Coffin Texts.* 3 vols. Warminster, England: Aris & Phillips, 1973.

———. *The Ancient Egyptian Pyramid Texts.* London: Oxford University Press, 1969.

———. *A Concise Dictionary of Middle Egyptian.* Oxford: Griffith Institute, 1981.

Fitzmyer, Joseph A. *The Genesis Apocryphon of Qumran Cave 1: A Commentary.* Rome: Pontifical Biblical Institute, 1966.

Fix, Wm. R. *Star Maps.* Toronto, Canada: Jonathan-James Books, 1979.

Frankfort, Henri. *Ancient Egyptian Religion.* New York: Harper Torchbooks, 1961.

Gardiner, Alan. *Egyptian Grammar.* 3d ed. London: Oxford University Press, 1969.

Griffiths, J. Gwyn. *The Origins of Osiris and His Cult.* Leiden, The Netherlands: E. J. Brill, 1980.

Hamilton, C. Mark, and Nina C. Cutrubus. *The Salt Lake Temple: A Monument to a People.* Salt Lake City: University Services, 1983.

Hamlyn, Paul. *Egyptian Mythology.* London: Westbrook House, 1965.

Harris, James R. "The Book of Abraham Facsimiles." *Studies in Scripture, Vol. 2: The Pearl of Great Price.* Edited by Robert L. Millet and Kent P. Jackson. Salt Lake City: Deseret Book, 1998.

———. *The Facsimiles of the Book of Abraham, A Study of the Joseph Smith Egyptian Papyri.* Payson, Utah: Harris House Publication, 1990.

Hart, George. *A Dictionary of Egyptian Gods and Goddesses.* Boston: Routledge and Kegan Paul, 1986.

Hornung, Erik. *Conceptions of God in Ancient Egypt.* Ithica, N.Y.: Cornell University Press, 1985.

Hunter, Milton R. *Pearl of Great Price Commentary.* Salt Lake City: Bookcraft, 1951.

Hymns of The Church of Jesus Christ of Latter-day Saints. Salt Lake City:

The Church of Jesus Christ of Latter-day Saints, 1985.

Jenkins, Nancy. *The Boat Beneath the Pyramid*. New York: Holt, Rinehart and Winston, 1980.

Journal of Discourses. 26 vols. London: Latter-day Saints' Book Depot, 1854–1886.

Keel, Othmar. *The Symbolism of the Biblical World*. New York: The Seabury Press, 1978.

La Farge, H. A. *Museums of Egypt*, Tokyo: Newsweek, Inc., and Kodansha Ltd., 1980.

Lamy, Lucie. *Egyptian Mysteries*. New York: Crossroad, 1981.

Ludlow, Daniel H. *A Companion to Your Study of the Book of Mormon*. Salt Lake City: Deseret Book, 1976.

Lund, Gerald N. *Selected Writings of Gerald N. Lund*. Salt Lake City: Deseret Book, n.d.

Lurker, Manfred. *The Gods and Symbols of Ancient Egypt*. London: Thomas and Hudson, 1980.

Lyon, Michael. *Appreciating Hypocephali as Words of Art and Faith*. Provo, Utah: F.A.R.M.S., 1999.

Madsen, Truman G., ed. *The Temple in Antiquity: Ancient Records and Modern Perspectives*. Provo, Utah: Religious Studies Center, Brigham Young University, 1984.

McConkie, Bruce, R. *Mormon Doctrine*. 2d ed. Salt Lake City: Bookcraft, 1966.

Mercer, Samuel A. B. *An Egyptian Grammar—with Chrestomathy and Glossary*. New York: Frederick Ungar Publishing, 1961.

Montet, P. *Everyday Life in Egypt*. Philadelphia: University of Pennsylvania Press, 1981.

Morenz, Siegfried. *Egyptian Religion*. Translated by Ann E. Keep. New York: Connell University Press, 1960.

Nibley, Hugh. "A New Look at the Pearl of Great Price," *Improvement Era*. Salt Lake City: The Church of Jesus Christ of Latter-day Saints," January 1968 to May 1970.

———. "As Things Stand at the Moment," *BYU Studies* 9 (Autumn 1968).

———. *Abraham in Egypt*. Salt Lake City: Deseret Book, 1981.

———. *Ancient Documents and the Pearl of Great Price*. Edited by Robert Smith and Robert Smythe. Provo, Utah: F.A.R.M.S., 1986.

———. "Facsimile No. 2." Forum, Ricks College, Rexburg, Idaho,

September 27, 1990.

———. *Figure 6 of Facsimile 2.* Provo, Utah: F.A.R.M.S., 1995.

———. *Lehi in the Desert/The World of the Jaredites/There Were Jaredites.* Edited by John W. Welch, Darrell L. Matthews, and Stephen R. Callister. Salt Lake City: Deseret Book and Provo, Utah: F.A.R.M.S., 1988.

———. *Old Testament and Related Studies.* Edited by John W. Welch, Gary P. Gillum, and Don E. Norton. Salt Lake City: Deseret Book and Provo, Utah: F.A.R.M.S., 1986.

———. "One Eternal Round—The Significance of the Egyptian Hypocephalus." Lectures given June 27 to September 26, 1990, Brigham Young University, Provo, Utah, 1990.

———. *The Message of the Joseph Smith Papyri: An Egyptian Endowment.* Salt Lake City: Deseret Book, 1975.

———. *Teachings of the Book of Mormon—Semester 1: Transcripts of Lectures Presented to an Honors Book of Mormon Class at Brigham Young University, 1998–1999.* Provo, Utah: Founation for Ancient Research, 1990.

———. *The Temple in Antiquity.* Salt Lake City: Bookcraft, 1984.

———. *The Three Facsimiles from the Book of Abraham.* Provo, Utah: F.A.R.M.S., 1985.

Nibley, Preston. *Brigham Young: The Man and His Work.* 4th ed. Salt Lake City: Deseret Book, 1936.

Packer, Boyd K. *The Holy Temple.* Salt Lake City: Bookcraft, 1986.

Patrick, Richard. *All Colour Book of Egyptian Mythology.* London: Octopus Books Limited, 1972.

Peterson, Donl H. *The Story of the Book of Abraham.* Salt Lake City: Deseret Book, 1995.

———. *The Pearl of Great Price: A History and Commentary.* Salt Lake City: Deseret Book, 1987.

Peterson, Mark E. *Adam Who is He?* Salt Lake City: Deseret Book, 1976.

Petrie, W. M. Flinders. *Abydos—Part 1.* London: Kegan Paul, Trench, Trubner & Co., 1902.

Quirke, Stephen. *Ancient Egyptian Religion.* London: British Museum Press, 1992.

Rawlinson, George. *History of Ancient Egypt.* 2 vols. London: Longman, Green, and Co., 1881.

Reeves, Nicholas. *The Complete Tutankhamun*. London: Thames and Hudson, 1990.

Rhodes, Michael D. "A Translation and Commentary of the Joseph Smith Hypocephalus." *BYU Studies* 17, no. 2 (1976–1977).

———. *The Joseph Smith Hypocephalus . . . Seventeen Years Later*. Provo, Utah: F.A.R.M.S., 1994.

Rossiter, Evelyn. *The Book of the Dead, Papyri of Ani, Hunefer, Anhai*. London: Crown Publishers, 1979.

Saleh, Janine Monnet. *The Egyptian Antiquities of Zagreb (Yougoslavia)*. Paris: Mouten, 1970.

Sety, Omm, and Hanny Zeini. *Abydos: Holy City of Ancient Egypt*. Los Angeles: LL Company, 1981.

Silverman, David P. *Masterpieces of Tutankhamun*. New York: Abbeville Press, 1978.

Smith, Joseph Fielding. *Man, His Origin and Destiny*. Salt Lake City: Deseret Book, 1954.

Smith, Joseph. *History of The Church of Jesus Christ of Latter-day Saints*. 2d ed. rev., 7 vols. Edited by B. H. Roberts. Salt Lake City: Deseret Book, 1987.

———. *Joseph Smith's Egyptian Alphabet and Grammar*. Salt Lake City: Utah Lighthouse Ministry, 1966.

———. *Lectures on Faith*. Compiled by N. B. Lundwall. Salt Lake City: Bookcraft, n.d.

———. *Teachings of the Prophet Joseph Smith*. Compiled by Joseph Fielding Smith. Salt Lake City: Deseret Book, 1976.

Strong, James. *Strong's Exhaustive Concordance of the Bible*. Nashville, Tennessee: Crusade Bible Publishers, Inc., 1894.

Talmage, James E. *The House of the Lord*. Salt Lake City: Deseret Book, 1969.

The Book of Jasher. Salt Lake City: J. H. Parry & Company, 1887.

The Metropolitan Museum of Art. *Treasures of Tutankhamen*. Edited by Katharine Stoddert Gilbert. New York: Ballantine Books, 1976.

Tobin, Vincent Arieh. *Theological Principles of Egyptian Religion*. New York: Peter Lang, 1989.

Todd, Jay M. *The Saga of the Book of Abraham*. Salt Lake City: Deseret Book, 1969.

Watterson, B. *The Gods of Ancient Egypt*. New York: Facts on File Publications, 1984.

Wilkinson, Richard H. *The Complete Gods and Goddesses of Ancient Egypt.* New York: Thames & Hudson, 2003.

ABOUT THE AUTHOR

Allen J. Fletcher was born in 1942 in Lethbridge, Alberta, Canada, and was raised in the town of Magrath. He served a mission to the East Central States, serving in Kentucky and Tennessee from 1961 to 1963.

While attending Ricks College, Allen married Elaine Hardy of Stirling, Alberta. He then attended Brigham Young University, graduating in 1967 with a degree in speech and dramatic arts. After graduating, he went to work for the Church Educational System and served in various capacities in Canada and the United States until his retirement in August 2004.

Allen earned a master's degree from the University of Calgary in 1990, receiving the International EDUCOM Award for the promotion of computers in higher education with respect to Egyptian studies.

He has served in many Church callings and is currently a high councilor in the Lethbridge Alberta East Stake. He and his wife have seven children and eleven grandchildren.